THE THREATS

BY MICHAEL BURGAN

RAINTREE
STECK-VAUGHN
PUBLISHERS

Published by Raintree Steck-Vaughn Publishers, an imprint of Steck-Vaughn Company.

Based on CNN's landmark series COLD WAR.
COLD WAR was co-produced by JIP Productions and CNN Productions. The Executive Producers were Sir Jeremy Isaacs and Pat Mitchell. Courtesy of Cable News Network, A Time Warner Company. All rights reserved.

Developed by Turner Learning, Inc. and Creative Media Applications (CMA)

Writer: Michael Burgan
Editor: Matt Levine
Managing Editor: Audrey Schewe
Historical Consultant: Mark Kramer

Design: Fabia Wargin Design
Maps: Ortelius Design
Photo Researcher: Janet Lankford

Raintree Steck-Vaughn Publishers Staff
Publishing Director: Walter Kossmann
Art Director: Max Brinkmann
Editors: Shirley Shalit, Sean Dolan

Library of Congress Cataloging-in-Publication Data
Burgan, Michael.
    The Cold War / by Michael Burgan.
       p. cm.
    Includes bibliographical references and index.
    Contents: [1] The separation — [2] The hot conflicts — [3] The threats — [4] The collapse.
    ISBN 0-7398-1834-1 (v. 1) — ISBN 0-7398-1835-X (v. 2) — ISBN 0-7398-1836-8 (v. 3) — ISBN 0-7398-1837-6 (v. 4)
       1. Cold war—Juvenile literature. 2. World politics—1945–1989—Juvenile literature. 3. United States—Foreign relations—Juvenile literature. 4. Soviet Union—Foreign relations—United States—Juvenile literature. 5. Post-communism—Juvenile literature. 6. Espionage, Russian—United States—Juvenile literature. 7. Espionage, American—Soviet Union—Juvenile literature. [1. Cold war. 2. World politics—1945–1989. 3. United States—Foreign relations. 4. Soviet Union—Foreign relations—United States.] I. Title.

D843 .B746 2001
909.82—dc21   00-062652

Printed and bound in the United States of America
1 2 3 4 5 6 7 8 9 0 (LB) 05 04 03 02 01

Acknowledgements
The author would like to thank the following people for their help and patience:
Lary Rosenblatt, Audrey Schewe, Matt Levine, Mark Kramer, Fabia Wargin, and Walter Kossmann. Special thanks to Thomas Paterson, for encouraging my love of history, and to Samantha, for everything.

Photo credits
Cover photos: (top) ©*Semyon Raskin/Magnum Photos*; (bottom left to right) *Archive Photos, Archive Photos, Blanche/Shone/Liaison*

© *AP/Wide World Photos:* 1, 17, 18, 24, 67, 71, 72, 73, 79, 87, 101.

© *CNN Productions:* 5, 7, 10, 12, 13, 15, 17, 19, 20, 23, 25, 29, 34, 36, 38, 41, 42, 44, 45, 47, 50, 51, 54, 55, 56, 58, 61, 64, 66, 75, 76, 83, 89, 92, 93, 94, 95, 96, 98, 99, 100, 108, 114.

© *Corbis Images:* 11, 36, 84, 112.

Courtesy *Department of Defense:* 43

Courtesy *U.S. Air Force:* 61

Courtesy *United States Senate Historical Office:* 69

THE THREATS

Table of Contents

INTRODUCTION 4

1 NEW LEADERS, OLD TENSIONS 5

2 FROM NUCLEAR TO THERMONUCLEAR 17

3 STIRRINGS IN THE EAST 29

4 INTO SPACE 41

5 GOOD TIMES AND BAD 55

6 COLD WAR HOME FRONT 67

7 THE WALL 83

8 MISSILES IN CUBA 99

TIME LINE 115

GLOSSARY 117

BIBLIOGRAPHY 121

INDEX 125

Introduction

A key year in the Cold War was 1953. The death of Joseph Stalin led to important changes in the leadership of the Soviet Union. Gradually Nikita Khrushchev emerged as the country's most powerful political force. During his rule, relations with the United States sometimes improved, but then took a step back as new international tensions arose. Soviet citizens experienced some improvement in their lives compared to when Stalin ruled, but the Communist party remained the sole authority.

Another new leader came to power in 1953—U.S. president Dwight Eisenhower. He helped bring an end to the Korean War and led the United States during a time of great economic growth. He also saw a continuing Soviet threat against American interests and pushed for the development of more and better *nuclear* weapons. But at times Eisenhower was eager to talk with Khrushchev to try to improve relations.

Eisenhower was followed in 1961 by John F. Kennedy. During Kennedy's brief presidency, the world experienced the two most frightening moments of the Cold War. Old problems in Berlin led to the building of a huge wall that divided the city in two—one side tied to America and the West, the other to the Communists of the East. Conflict along the wall in 1961 brought U.S. and Soviet tanks just yards away from each other. Then, in 1962 the Soviet Union tried to assert itself in the Western Hemisphere by secretly bringing nuclear weapons to Cuba. The Cuban Missile Crisis that followed posed the risk of nuclear war.

Luckily for the world, each crisis ended peacefully. Both the United States and the Soviet Union knew that if they used their nuclear weapons, they might kill millions of people in just a few minutes. Still, the threat of nuclear war always seemed close as each side continued to distrust its Cold War foe.

NEW LEADERS, OLD TENSIONS

1

Dwight D. Eisenhower became U.S. president in January 1953. He soon began looking for ways to end the Korean War, which had started almost three years earlier. Eisenhower also tried to create his own strategies for dealing with the Soviet Union, America's Communist opponent in the Cold War. He could not know that events halfway around the world would have immediate, profound effects on the Cold War.

Soviet officials carry the casket of Joseph Stalin during his funeral in 1953.

On March 5, a few days after suffering a stroke, Joseph Stalin died. As the leader of the Soviet Union for 25 years, Stalin had turned the country into a *superpower*. He had created modern industries and led the Soviet Union through World War II. Said one Moscow resident, "We thought of Stalin as our father who would always look after us."

But Stalin also had an evil side. In his drive for absolute power, he had committed terrible acts of violence and terror against his own people. Stalin's policies and the brutal tactics of his secret police had resulted in the death and imprisonment of tens of millions of Soviet citizens.

In Washington, Eisenhower and his aides debated what Stalin's death would mean for relations between the United States and the Soviet Union. In April the president said the Soviet Union had disrupted world peace in the past, but he hoped that the two superpowers could have friendlier relations. Eisenhower noted the high cost of the military rivalry created by the Cold War: "Every gun that is made, every warship launched, every rocket fired signifies, in the final sense, a theft from those who hunger and are not fed."

However, Eisenhower's remarks were not a signal that the Cold War was over. His secretary of state, John Foster Dulles, said,

"We are not dancing to any Russian tune." A few months earlier, Dulles had told Congress that the United States should not be willing just to contain *communism*. Under President Harry S. Truman, a Democrat, *containment* had been the official U.S. policy. Dulles pledged that he would try to free countries that were under Soviet influence. He said, "A policy which only aims at containing Russia... is an unsound policy.... If our only policy is to stay where we are, we will be driven back. It is only by keeping alive the hope of liberation, by taking advantage of that wherever opportunity arises, that we will end this terrible peril which dominates the world."

People   JOHN FOSTER DULLES

To many outside observers, John Foster Dulles was a dedicated supporter of U.S. Cold War policies. He saw a sharp divide between "godless communism" and the values of the United States. But as government records show, Dulles actually had a more sophisticated view of the struggles of the Cold War. He recognized that the Soviet Union changed some of its thinking after Stalin's death, and he saw the importance of negotiating with Nikita Khrushchev. Dulles talked about "rolling back" communism, but he was willing to stick with the old policy of merely containing it.

Dulles was born on February 25, 1888, in Washington, D.C. Both his grandfather (John Foster) and his uncle (Robert Lansing) served for a time as U.S. secretary of state. While still in college, Dulles attended an international peace conference with his grandfather and saw firsthand the workings of diplomacy. After finishing law school, Dulles worked as a lawyer specializing in international issues.

After World War II, Dulles was one of the Republican advisors who helped shape the foreign policy of a Democratic president, Harry Truman. Dulles supported the creation of the United Nations (UN), and in 1951 Truman selected him to negotiate a treaty with Japan. But during the 1952 presidential campaign, Dulles sharply attacked Truman's Cold War policies, especially containment. When Dwight Eisenhower won the election, he chose Dulles as his secretary of state.

Dulles helped Eisenhower shape a new Cold War policy known as *massive retaliation*. Under this policy the United States would put more of its resources into developing nuclear arms—and would use them if the Soviet Union threatened vital U.S. interests. Despite the tough talk, Dulles was cool during the many crises of the era, and the United States avoided direct conflicts with the Soviet Union. In 1958 Dulles was diagnosed with terminal cancer. He retired as secretary of state shortly after and died on May 24, 1959.

Changes in Moscow

In the Soviet Union, the leaders of the Communist party had a more immediate problem than trying to deal with current U.S. policies. Stalin had not indicated who should come after him as leader. The Communist party, not the Soviet people, held ultimate power, and a group of senior party officials ruled the country after Stalin died. The top leaders included Georgi Malenkov as the prime minister and Lavrenti Beria as his deputy and head of state security. Vyacheslav Molotov was restored to his post as foreign minister and Nikolai Bulganin was minister of defense. Another top leader was Nikita Khrushchev, a high-ranking party official.

The new leadership seemed to bring a new attitude toward the Cold War. While serving under Stalin, Malenkov had been a loyal party member who helped carry out some of the massacres of the Great Terror. Now, he was still committed to Communist rule, but he favored easing some of the harsh methods Stalin had used. Malenkov talked about improving relations with the West. In one of his first speeches, he said, "There is no disputed or unsolved question which could not be settled by peaceful means with any foreign country, including the United States." The new attitude toward the Americans was called *peaceful coexistence.* Vladimir Lenin, the founder of the Soviet regime, had first used the phrase decades earlier.

Malenkov and the other Soviet leaders wanted to end the Korean War. They pressured North Korean leader Kim Il Sung to make peace, and the war finally ended in July 1953. But within the ruling Soviet leadership, the situation was not always so peaceful. The leaders scrambled among themselves to see who would wield the most power, both in the government and in the Communist party. Malenkov was stripped of his title as a secretary of the party, though he still remained a high-ranking official. Within six months Khrushchev was appointed first secretary, the top position in the party. The leaders were divided along several lines, but gradually most of them joined forces against Beria. The tensions within the leadership rose as problems developed in East Germany.

In the Image of Stalin

Officially called the German Democratic Republic (GDR), East Germany was created after the Berlin crisis of 1948 ended the following year. The country was one of the Soviet Union's *satellite* states in Eastern Europe. Since the end of World War II, Germany had been a major concern for the Soviet Union and its former Western allies—Great Britain, France, and the United States. Germany was now split in two, and West Germany was aligned with the Western powers. Berlin, the German capital, was also carved in half, with one side under Communist control and the other under Western control.

The leader of East Germany was Walter Ulbricht. A loyal follower of Stalin, he exercised the same tight control over his country that Stalin had used in the Soviet Union. Ulbricht's secret police, the Stasi, kept close watch on East German citizens and encouraged people to spy on friends and neighbors. Ulbricht also wanted East Germany to become an industrial power as quickly as possible. Stalin had favored this, as well, since much of East Germany's iron and steel production ended up in the Soviet Union.

Most East Germans at the time faced harsh living conditions. Alfred Berlin, a construction worker, said, "The average person lived very badly.... [H]eating, coal, electricity, these things were all rationed. Electricity for domestic use was simply not available. The morale of the population dropped to zero." Ulbricht's demands that the people work harder also drained their morale.

These East Germans prepare to head to the West through West Berlin.

East German citizens did have one way to improve their lives: by fleeing to the West. West Berlin was a small oasis of freedom in the middle of East Germany, and people could still freely enter the western half of the city from East Berlin. Living conditions were not always the best for these *refugees*, but they were thankful to escape Ulbricht's rule.

During the spring of 1953, the number of East Germans flocking to the West reached nearly 15,000 per month. Ulbricht further tightened his control over the GDR, which alarmed Soviet leaders. The new leaders in Moscow had been encouraging the Eastern European satellites to ease some of their more restrictive policies. The Soviet Union also had a special interest in East Germany. Soviet officials were considering a new policy: pushing for East and West Germany to reunite, but as a neutral state, with no ties to either the United States or the Soviet Union. Soviet leaders ordered Ulbricht to relax some of his social and economic controls. Ulbricht reluctantly agreed, but he continued to force industrial workers to produce at high levels.

People — WALTER ULBRICHT

After World War II, when Joseph Stalin selected leaders for his Eastern European satellites, he wanted loyal Communists who would follow Moscow's orders. The man he picked for East Germany was Walter Ulbricht.

Born on June 30, 1893, in Leipzig, Germany, Ulbricht joined his first socialist group when he was a teenager. During World War I, he joined the Spartacus League, a radical group that eventually became the German Communist party. Ulbricht was a dedicated party worker. In 1922 he made his first trip to Moscow, where he met the Communist leader of the Soviet Union, Vladimir Lenin. Later, Ulbricht joined the Communist International (Comintern),

the Soviet Union's tool for spreading communism around the world. He faithfully followed Joseph Stalin—even in 1932 when Stalin ordered the German Communists to help unseat the democratic government then in power.

Once Adolf Hitler took power, German Communists were considered enemies of the state, and Ulbricht soon left Germany. From 1935 to April 1945, he lived in Moscow and became the most influential German Communist. He returned to Germany near the end of World War II to set up a Communist party in Soviet-occupied territory. Ulbricht eventually won control of the socialist movement in eastern Germany and readily carried out Stalin's wishes.

Stalin's death created problems for Ulbricht because the new Soviet leaders disagreed with his policies. After holding on to his power through the Berlin crisis of 1953, Ulbricht continued his strict rule over East Germany. He served until 1971, when Soviet leaders forced him from office. Ulbricht died on August 1, 1973.

The Breaking Point in Berlin

On June 16, 1953, opposition to Ulbricht's policies peaked. In East Berlin workers protested in the streets and called for other workers across the country to go on strike. Said Charles Wheeler, a British journalist in Berlin, "[B]y that time, striking itself was a political act, was an act of rebellion, but marching through the streets was something more. It was almost kicking off a revolution."

A Soviet tank rumbles through East Berlin to end an anti-government protest.

The next day 60,000 marchers filled the streets of East Berlin, and hundreds of thousands more protested in other East German cities. Alarmed by the growing unrest, the Soviet leadership ordered Soviet tanks stationed in East Germany to roll into action and save Ulbricht's government from collapse. Heinz Homuth, one of the protesters, later recalled, "We couldn't do anything against the tanks with our bare hands and stones. As soon as the firing started, people began to drop down, wounded or dead.... For us, the dream of freedom was over." At least 40 people were killed and more than 400 were injured. Thousands more were arrested. Smaller demonstrations went on for a few more days, but the Soviet soldiers eventually restored order across East Germany.

Publicly East German and Soviet leaders accused the United States of stirring the protests. Allen Dulles, head of the U.S. *Central Intelligence Agency* (CIA)—and brother of John Foster Dulles—said in private, "The United States had nothing whatsoever to do with inciting these riots." RIAS, the American radio station in West Berlin, had even broadcast announcements telling people to remain calm during the crisis. Despite their earlier talk of rolling back communism, Eisenhower and Secretary of State Dulles did not want to get involved in East Berlin. In their own records, East German and Soviet leaders admitted that Ulbricht's policies had provoked the unrest.

Sources   A JOURNALIST'S VIEW

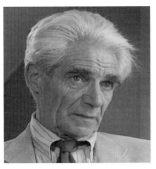

Charles Wheeler

In 1953 Charles Wheeler was a reporter for the British Broadcasting Company (BBC) in West Berlin. He witnessed the crisis of that year. Here, he describes some of the events of June 17.

[T]here was a line of People's Policemen in blue uniforms, with truncheons [clubs], and as the leaders of this quite small march reached the People's Police, there was an immediate confrontation. The people at the back were pushing, the people at the front were trying to stop, and the People's Police started hitting them with truncheons. That was the first clash. But more and more people came in from outside, from factories in

the suburbs and so on and gradually a very large crowd was roaming around the center of Berlin...and then suddenly we saw the first Soviet tanks. And I remember saying to some...little group of people I was with, don't worry, they're firing in blanks and at that point a brick fell off a wall behind me. They were not firing blanks, they were firing live ammunition, but not at the demonstrators at that point, over their heads. And then, about an hour later, a large crowd assembled in a large square...when four Russian tanks drove into the square, four abreast, and went straight for the crowd. And I remember one man got caught and was run over by a tank and everybody stampeded and people were knocked over....*

A New Leader Emerges

A few weeks after calm had been restored to East Germany, Ulbricht traveled to Moscow to confer with the Soviet leaders. Despite his earlier policies that had troubled Soviet government, Ulbricht remained in power.

Missing at the Moscow gathering was Beria. He had been arrested on June 26. He was accused of "anti-party and anti-state activities." In reality Beria and the other Soviet leaders had few major differences in policy. But the lack of a single strong leader after Stalin's death created tensions, and Beria's control of the secret police led to suspicions about his intentions. Beria's energy in suggesting new policies in the spring of 1953 deepened those suspicions.

Khrushchev's son, Sergei, described his father's fears, saying that Khrushchev thought "especially after Stalin's death, that if they will not take Beria out of power...it will be a threat [to the] life of all of the others, because they will be arrested and eliminated. So, until the last days, he [acted] very friendly himself to Beria [but on] the other side, he plotted against him and plotted successfully."

Khrushchev secured the support of Malenkov, who had previously aligned himself with Beria. He also gained the backing of a leading Soviet military officer, Georgi Zhukov. "The military hated Beria," said Soviet scholar Vladislav Zubok. "They viewed him as part of the machine that had murdered so many able officers in the 1930s and '40s." After his arrest Beria was held prisoner until his execution in December 1953.

With Beria gone Khrushchev gradually emerged as the leader of the Soviet Union. But it took a few years for Khrushchev to achieve clear-cut supremacy—and for the United States to realize that he was in control.

People ☭ NIKITA KHRUSHCHEV

As leader of the Soviet Union, Nikita Khrushchev was a complex person. He called for peaceful coexistence with the United States, yet he often threatened the use of Soviet nuclear might. He allowed some reforms in Eastern Europe but cracked down when the reforms went too far. In the end he was too *liberal* and too unstable for other leading Soviet Communists, and they forced him from power.

Nikita Sergeyevich Khrushchev was born on April 17, 1894, in the village of Kalnikova in Ukraine. His family was poor and uneducated, and they eventually moved to a nearby industrial center. While working in factories, Khrushchev helped organize strikes to protest working conditions. After the *Bolshevik* takeover in 1917, he joined the Soviet Communist party.

During the 1920s Khrushchev was a Communist party official in Ukraine, which was then part of the Soviet Union. He backed Joseph Stalin in his campaigns against other Soviet Communist leaders. When Stalin emerged on top, he rewarded Khrushchev with increasingly important positions in the party. In 1939 Khrushchev was named to the party's ruling body, the Politburo. He supported Stalin's Great Terror of the 1930s, betraying Soviet citizens and willingly accepting the murder of Ukrainian intellectuals.

From the late 1930s until 1949, Khrushchev was the Communist party leader in Ukraine. He oversaw the torture and murder of citizens who defied the Communist party. After returning to Moscow, he became one of Stalin's top advisors and was one of the small group of Communists who took control after Stalin's death in 1953. Khrushchev was named head of the Communist party later that year and eventually became the Soviet Union's supreme leader. He served until 1964, when he was removed from office.

Looking back on his time as the leader of the Soviet Union, Khrushchev wrote, "We [Soviet leaders and U.S. leaders] couldn't agree then, and we can't agree now.... Maybe it's impossible for us to agree." He died on September 11, 1971.

Espionage THE "UNDERWORLD" OF SPYING

East Berlin was a center for communications between Soviet forces in Eastern Europe and Soviet leaders in Moscow. After the 1953 East German crisis, the United States and Britain took advantage of this situation. In 1954 they secretly dug a tunnel from West Berlin into East Berlin and tapped into Soviet communication lines. But from the very beginning of the tunnel project, Soviet officials knew about it. George Blake, a British intelligence officer in Berlin, was also spying for the Soviet Union.

Soviet officials did not want the West to know they knew about the tunnel. Shutting it down right away might have tipped off the West that one of their own people was working against them. Instead, Soviet officials allowed the tunnel to remain open for about a year. Thanks to the tunnel, U.S. and British intelligence learned about Soviet military operations in Eastern Europe. They also picked up information on Soviet spies.

Finally in 1956 the Soviet Union shut down the tunnel and denounced the West for its *espionage* activities. Blake continued to spy for the Soviet Union until 1961 when he was arrested by British officials. Sentenced to jail for 42 years, he later escaped, but he was recaptured and returned to jail.

2

FROM NUCLEAR TO THERMONUCLEAR

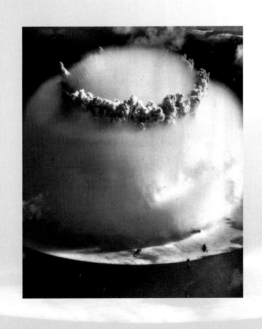

A cloud rises from the 1946 test explosion of a nuclear bomb in the Marshall Islands, where the United States later tested its first hydrogen bomb.

Days before Dwight Eisenhower was elected president in November 1952, the United States tested a new weapon, the *hydrogen bomb* (H-bomb). Also called a *thermonuclear bomb*, a hydrogen bomb relies on a process called *fusion* to create enormous amounts of energy. Atoms from *radioactive* materials are *fused*, or joined together. Fusion produces temperatures at least as hot as the core of the sun. Nuclear bombs, first exploded in 1945, use *fission* to create their destructive power. During fission the *nuclei*, or cores, of radioactive atoms are split apart, releasing energy.

The world's first hydrogen bomb was tested in the remote Marshall Islands in the Pacific Ocean. Its explosive force was 500 times more powerful than the nuclear bomb that the United States had dropped on Hiroshima, Japan, in World War II. Harold Agnew, a U.S. nuclear physicist, was at the test. "You don't know what heat is," he said, "until you've seen the heat from a 10–megaton hydrogen bomb. It doesn't stop, it just gets hotter and hotter and you start to really worry even though you're 20-some miles away.... [T]he whole island disappeared too...and the whole lagoon was just sort of milky white."

Not everyone in America welcomed the development of the H-bomb. Physicist J. Robert Oppenheimer had worked on the "Manhattan Project," the U.S. wartime effort to build a nuclear bomb. In 1949 he led a committee that recommended that President Harry Truman not approve building the H-bomb. The committee said the so-called "super bomb" was "an evil thing considered in any light." Critics like Oppenheimer believed it was wrong to develop this kind of weapon during peacetime. In their view, doing so would only fuel competition with the Soviet Union to have the most destructive weapons, creating an arms race.

One of the scientists who helped build the first nuclear bomb, J. Robert Oppenheimer opposed U.S. efforts to build a "super bomb."

Despite these concerns Truman approved the development of the hydrogen bomb. He believed that the United States had to be in a position of strength during its dealings with the Soviet Union. Because the Soviet government had tested its own nuclear bomb in 1949, the United States had to stay one step ahead with the hydrogen bomb. Now, in 1953 Dwight Eisenhower was the president who would have to consider when and if the United States would ever use this powerful new bomb.

The Bomb · BUILDING THE SUPER BOMB

Many scientists worked to harness the power of nuclear fusion. But the United States and the Soviet Union each have one man who is often considered the "father" of the H-bomb. In the United States, it is

Edward Teller. In the Soviet Union, it is Andrei Sakharov.

Teller and his colleague, Stanislaw Ulam, found a way to use a small fission bomb to power a hydrogen bomb. The explosion from a fission device created the intense pressure and energy needed to fuse together hydrogen atoms and create a thermonuclear reaction. This reaction created immense amounts of destructive energy. Sakharov, working at the same time in the Soviet Union, came up with a similar process. The hydrogen bomb was vastly more powerful than the fission bombs developed at the end of World War II. It was also cheaper to make, in the sense that it produced more explosive power for every dollar spent.

Outside the lab Teller and Sakharov were both outspoken scientists. Teller was a strong anti-Communist and called for new weapons to give the United States a military advantage over the Soviet Union. In the early 1960s, Sakharov began to speak out against the use of nuclear weapons and their testing. For this and other views that contradicted official Soviet polices, he was later sent to jail.

Massive Retaliation

A huge mushroom-shaped cloud hovers above the testing site of a Soviet thermonuclear bomb.

Long before the United States had started its super bomb project, the Soviet Union had been working on a thermonuclear bomb. In August 1953 the Soviet military tested its first.

The Soviet thermonuclear bomb got most of its explosive power from fission, not fusion; scientists do not consider it a true fusion bomb. The Soviet thermonuclear bomb was smaller than the U.S. bomb, making it easier to transport. This meant that the Soviet bomb was potentially easier to drop on enemy forces.

The new Soviet weapons concerned Eisenhower and Secretary of State Dulles. They began to develop a new strategy for dealing with growing Soviet military strength. U.S. officials doubted that the Soviet Union would deliberately start a nuclear war. But they believed that Soviet leaders felt confident enough to respond with force if they thought the United States was threatening their interests. The United States had to be prepared to react quickly and powerfully to any Soviet attack. This strategy, it was hoped, would *deter*, or prevent, a Soviet attack in the first place.

However, Eisenhower did not want to spend huge sums of money on defense. He wanted to have the strongest forces possible for the least amount of money. In the everyday language of the time, this was called "more bang for the buck." This approach led to an increasing U.S. reliance on nuclear weapons as part of any American counterattack. The overall strategy was called massive retaliation.

In January 1954 Dulles explained massive retaliation to the American people. Local military defenses, he said, "must be reinforced by the further deterrent of massive retaliatory power.... The way to deter aggression is for the free community to be willing and able to respond vigorously at places and with means of its own choosing."

| Sources | NUCLEAR PLANNING |

In 1953 President Eisenhower's military advisors drafted a secret policy for U.S. relations with the Soviet Union and the possible use of nuclear weapons. This document, called NSC-162/2, was adopted on October 30, 1953. It was the basis for the U.S. policy of massive retaliation. Here are some excerpts from NSC-162/2.

The capability of the USSR to attack the United States with atomic weapons has been continuously growing and will be materially enhanced by hydrogen weapons. The USSR has sufficient bombs and aircraft, using one-way missions, to inflict serious damage on the United States, especially by surprise attack. The USSR soon may have the capability of dealing a crippling blow to our industrial base and our continued ability to prosecute a war....

Within the free world, only the United States can provide and maintain, for a period of years to come, the atomic capability to counterbalance Soviet atomic power. Thus, sufficient atomic weapons and effective means of delivery are indispensable for U.S. security....

In the event of hostilities, the United States will consider nuclear weapons to be as available for use as other munitions....

Technology   NUCLEAR POWER UNDER THE SEA

Although the power of nuclear fission was first used in weapons, many scientists realized that nuclear power had other possible uses. Scientist and U.S. Navy captain Hyman Rickover thought that a nuclear-powered submarine would revolutionize underwater warfare. He proved to be right. The result of Rickover's idea was the USS *Nautilus*.

The *Nautilus*, the world's first nuclear submarine, was launched in January 1954. Using a nuclear-powered engine, the sub could remain underwater for months at a time, using very little fuel. Under the sea the *Nautilus* cruised at more than 20 miles (32 km) per hour for long stretches. Non-nuclear subs relied on batteries to travel underwater. They could go only short distances at much slower speeds. In 1958, traveling under thick sheets of ice, the *Nautilus* became the first vessel to cross the North Pole.

Nuclear submarines played an important role during the Cold War. The United States and the Soviet Union equipped their nuclear subs with nuclear missiles. The vessels were constantly on patrol. They offered either side a chance to strike back with a large nuclear force if its enemy launched a surprise attack on land-based missiles. The nuclear engine of the *Nautilus* also had a peaceful impact. Its design led to nuclear power plants that supply electricity for civilian use.

Preparing for War

The United States had already selected thousands of potential targets within the Soviet Union. The U.S. military was also developing small nuclear weapons, called *tactical nuclear weapons*, that could be used on the battlefield.

Duck and Cover #1

Bombers were now an increasingly important part of the U.S. nuclear arsenal. Starting in 1953 the U.S. Air Force received 40 percent of the country's total military budget. The next year the United States still faced a technological challenge. It needed H-bombs that could be dropped from its bombers.

The Soviet Union was also preparing for future nuclear combat. In September 1954 the Soviet military dropped a nuclear bomb into an area where Soviet military training was held. After the blast Soviet troops practiced their fighting skills. This was part of their training to fight a nuclear war. Valentin Larionov, a Soviet general, attended this exercise. "I remember well," he said, "how Marshal Bulganin, the minister of defense, stated that, 'Nuclear weapons were not as frightening as we had been warned by [the West].'"

Soldiers on both sides were not the only people preparing for war. In the United States, the government promoted *civil defense*—the steps civilians should take in case of war. Civil defense included drills to prepare for a nuclear attack. In one drill in 1953, 600 air-raid sirens called New York City residents to underground *bomb shelters*. Within minutes the normally crowded streets were practically deserted.

In schools children learned to "duck and cover" in case of a nuclear attack. One student of the time recalled,

The U.S. government created the cartoon character Bert the Turtle to help teach children to "duck and cover" in case of a nuclear attack.

"We would get out under our desks and stay there until we were told to come out or, in some cases, we'd get our coats and we'd go out into the hallways and we would literally duck down facing the wall." Duck-and-cover tactics probably would not have saved many people from a real nuclear blast, but the drills gave people some hope that they could survive.

People   CURTIS LEMAY

"Bombs away with Curtis LeMay." That rhyming slogan first appeared when General Curtis LeMay took over America's strategy for bombing Japan at the end of World War II. During the first years of the Cold War, LeMay was in charge of the *Strategic Air Command* (SAC), the branch of the air force given the task of dropping nuclear bombs if they were ever needed in combat.

LeMay was born on November 15, 1906, in Columbus, Ohio. He began flying planes for the military during the 1920s. In World War II, LeMay led bomber planes on missions over Germany before taking over the bombing command in the Pacific. LeMay came up with the strategy to drop incendiary bombs from low-flying bombers. These bombs unleashed destructive fires when they hit. One raid on Tokyo killed an estimated

100,000 civilians—higher than the death toll from the nuclear bomb dropped on Hiroshima.

When LeMay took charge of SAC in 1948, he immediately turned it into an efficient and important arm of U.S. defense. He wanted a huge arsenal of nuclear weapons so that the Soviet Union would not think of attacking first. If necessary LeMay's strategy was to have SAC "deliver the entire stockpile of atomic weapons, if made available, in a single massive attack." Under LeMay the SAC bomber force grew from about 600 planes in 1951 to more than 3,000 in 1959.

During the early years of the Vietnam War, LeMay was the air force chief of staff. He often clashed with his civilian bosses over how to conduct the air war in Vietnam. After leaving the military in 1965, LeMay unsuccessfully ran for vice president in 1968 with presidential candidate George Wallace, the governor of Alabama. Their *conservative* American Independent party opposed laws that promoted racial equality. LeMay died on October 1, 1990.

The Bomb — UNLUCKY DRAGON

In March 1954 the United States returned to the Marshall Islands to test its latest hydrogen bomb. This bomb was designed to be dropped from an airplane. American scientists calculated that the bomb's blast would equal the force of five million tons of dynamite. They also predicted how far the *radiation* produced by the blast—called *fallout*—would travel. But the scientists miscalculated. The blast was more than twice as large as they expected, and the fallout carried far out to sea, right into the path of the *Fukuryu Maru*.

The *Fukuryu Maru* (Japanese for "Lucky Dragon") was a fishing boat. After the hydrogen blast, the sailors onboard saw a huge light in the western sky. "Seven or eight minutes later," one sailor said, "there was a terrific sound—like an avalanche. Then a visible multi-colored ball of fire appeared on the horizon." The fallout from the blast rained down on the crew of the Lucky Dragon.

A victim of the Lucky Dragon *nuclear accident.*

All the sailors on the boat became sick from their exposure to radiation. One man died seven months later. The accident sparked a huge outcry in Japan. Many Japanese were already highly sensitive to the dangers of nuclear weapons and radiation because of the nuclear bombs dropped on their country during World War II. By August 1955, 32 million Japanese had signed a petition protesting further U.S. nuclear tests in the Pacific.

Today, the Lucky Dragon is preserved as a museum. About 300,000 visit it each year to learn about the accident of 1954.

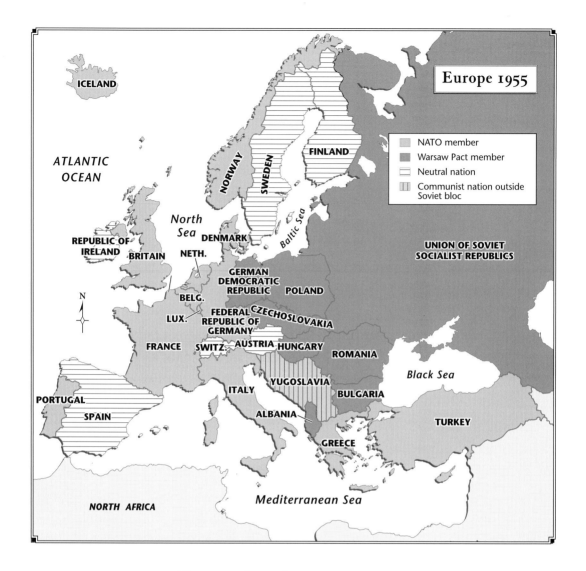

Europe 1955

NATO member
Warsaw Pact member
Neutral nation
Communist nation outside Soviet bloc

ICELAND

ATLANTIC
OCEAN

NORWAY

SWEDEN

FINLAND

Baltic Sea

North
Sea

DENMARK

REPUBLIC OF
IRELAND

BRITAIN

NETH.

UNION OF SOVIET
SOCIALIST REPUBLICS

GERMAN
DEMOCRATIC
REPUBLIC

POLAND

BELG.

LUX.

FEDERAL
REPUBLIC OF
GERMANY

CZECHOSLOVAKIA

N

FRANCE

SWITZ.

AUSTRIA

HUNGARY

ROMANIA

YUGOSLAVIA

ITALY

Black Sea

PORTUGAL

SPAIN

ALBANIA

BULGARIA

GREECE

TURKEY

NORTH AFRICA

Mediterranean Sea

Events in Europe

While the United States and the Soviet Union prepared for possible nuclear warfare, they also addressed some old issues. During the spring of 1955, a series of important events took place in Europe. In May the three Western Allies of World War II—Britain, France, and the United States—ended their military occupation of West Germany. They also agreed that the West Germans could have their own military forces—their first since the end of the war—and join the *North Atlantic Treaty Organization* (NATO).

By joining this military defense organization, West Germany became firmly tied to the West.

Also in May, the three Western Allies, along with the Soviet Union, ended their military occupation of Austria. The country had been taken over by Nazi Germany before World War II, and many Austrians supported the Nazis. After the war, the Allies had divided up Austria and sent in troops, as they did with Germany. Now, 40,000 Soviet troops and a much smaller force from the West were to leave. In return the Austrians pledged to remain neutral and not formally support either side in the Cold War.

Both the Soviet Union and the United States felt they had won a small victory with the agreement. Each would have preferred to have Austria in its own sphere of influence, but at least neither had "lost" Austria to its enemy. Secretary of State Dulles hoped that the pullout of Soviet troops would spark a new drive for freedom in the Soviet satellites of Eastern Europe. Within the Soviet government, Molotov opposed pulling out Soviet troops. But according to Soviet *diplomat* Anatoly Dobrynin, "[M]ost of the Soviet leaders disagreed with him and thought we have to make a goodwill gesture and start talks in Europe."

At the same time, the Soviet Union was starting its own military alliance to balance the existence of NATO. On May 14, leaders from the Eastern European satellites and the Soviet Union met in Warsaw, Poland, and signed the Warsaw Pact. In this treaty the countries pledged to defend one another in case of an attack or a threat to their security. The Soviet Union was clearly in charge of the pact and controlled the armies of the member states.

The Geneva Conference

Cold War tensions in Europe lessened as 1955 went on. In July, Eisenhower joined leaders from Britain, France, and the Soviet Union at a conference in Geneva, Switzerland. It was the first time a U.S. president had met with Soviet leaders in ten years, since the Potsdam Conference just before the end of World War II.

In Geneva the overall mood was friendly, though no major agreements were reached. Eisenhower spelled out a plan he called "Open Skies." Under the proposal, the Soviet Union and the United States would be free to fly over each other's territories and observe defense operations. Soviet leaders opposed the plan; Khrushchev called it "an espionage plot." Open Skies was mostly designed to make the United States look willing to pursue arms control—Eisenhower never really expected the Russians to accept it.

Some good things did come out of the conference. The world welcomed the positive mood at the conference—the so-called "spirit of Geneva." The Soviet Union and the United States agreed to some cultural exchanges. Citizens of each country could visit the other. And the Americans learned who was truly in charge of their Cold War foe. It was clearer than ever that Khrushchev was calling the shots for the Soviet Union.

Sources   IN GENEVA

During Dwight Eisenhower's first term as president, Robert Bowie served on the *National Security Council* (NSC) and the Policy Planning Staff of the State Department. Both groups advised the president on military and foreign policy issues. Here, Bowie discusses some of the aims of the Geneva Conference.

I think Eisenhower hoped maybe that something...of a small start [might be] made on arms control, or disarmament. I think he hoped in any event to have an opportunity to convince the...Soviet leaders that nuclear war was suicidal and it was just something that must be avoided and that therefore there was a common interest, a shared interest, in trying to achieve ways to make sure that no nuclear war happened by accident or otherwise.... And finally I think Eisenhower in particular was anxious to see more interchange, he strongly favored more trade, really, with the Soviets than most of the people in the administration, just because he thought any kind of interchange, any kind of flow back and forth would have the effect...of exposing the Soviet system to outside influences of some sort.

3

STIRRINGS
IN THE
EAST

North
Sea

Baltic Sea

Crisis between Soviet and
Polish leadership ends
peacefully late October

Poznań

Warsaw

POLAND

EAST
GERMANY

Polish troops crush
protests June 29

WEST
GERMANY

CZECHOSLOVAKIA

Soviet troops enter Oct 24
Hungarian uprising crushed
November 4

Budapest

HUNGARY

N

Stirrings in the East
June–November 1956

I n 1955 the top Soviet leaders still included Georgi Malenkov, Vyacheslav Molotov, and Nikolai Bulganin. But in the public eye, Nikita Khrushchev had emerged as the "first among equals." In May, Khrushchev went to Yugoslavia to try to improve relations with that Communist country. Its leader, Josip Broz Tito, had broken away from Soviet influence in 1948. Under Stalin, Yugoslavia was seen as a traitor to the Communist cause.

Khrushchev made other trips abroad, as well. He visited so-called "Third World" countries, most of them newly independent after being ruled by European powers. These countries, located primarily in Africa and Asia, were poor compared to the West, and many had not yet chosen to support either the United States or the Soviet Union. Khrushchev hoped to promote *socialism* (the economic system practiced by the Communists) in these countries and gain allies for the Soviet Union. On his trips he received warm welcomes.

Khrushchev was also asserting his authority within the Soviet Communist party. As head of the party, he pressured Malenkov into resigning as Soviet premier in February 1955. A year later at the 20th Congress of the Soviet Communist party, Khrushchev stunned the party with a "secret speech" that attacked the former self-proclaimed hero of Soviet communism, Joseph Stalin.

The "Secret" Speech

Before 1956, national Communist party meetings were usually highly staged. The party leaders made predictable speeches about the strength of the party and where it was going. At a public session in February 1956, Khrushchev upset the expected routine with a controversial speech. He went against the traditional ideas of Stalin and suggested that Communist countries did not have to defeat capitalist countries in war to spread socialism. Communist countries led by the Soviet Union, he argued, were now strong enough to spread their ideas through peaceful means.

Khrushchev saved his biggest shock for the end of the 20th Congress. Behind closed doors he denounced the past policies of Stalin. He detailed the horrible tactics Stalin had used to ensure his absolute control of the Soviet Union, imprisoning and killing thousands of party members. (Khrushchev did not talk about the millions of non-party members also massacred under Stalin.) Before this speech no one had dared criticize Stalin and his tactics at a party congress. Said one observer at the congress, "When he made his speech, people in the hall started to groan. There were shouts of 'Shame!'"

Many of the party members in the room, including Khrushchev, had eagerly carried out Stalin's orders. They did not want to acknowledge the crimes they had committed. Others, however, sensed that Khrushchev was pointing out a new direction for the Soviet Union. They hoped that it would be possible to tell the truth more often, instead of covering up terrible deeds.

Copies of this secret speech were given to party members. A copy ended up in the hands of the CIA, which used Khrushchev's attack on Stalin as propaganda against the Soviet system. The contents of the speech were broadcast on Radio Free Europe, a U.S. radio service beamed into Eastern Europe. The service was designed to spread propaganda against communism and encourage listeners to support *democracy*. Jan Nowak worked on Radio Free Europe broadcasts for Poland. In recalling the effect of Khrushchev's speech on the Communist party members who heard it, he said, "[T]he party people...were led to believe, and they did believe, that Stalin is God, that he...couldn't make any mistake.... [T]heir faith, their religion, collapsed."

Sources ☭ KHRUSHCHEV CRITICIZES STALIN

Here are selections from Khrushchev's speech to the 20th Congress of the Soviet Communist party.

Stalin showed in a whole series of cases his intolerance, his brutality and his abuse of power.... He often chose the path of repression and annihilation, not only against actual enemies, but also against individuals who had not committed any crimes against the party and the Soviet government....

Stalin was a very distrustful man.... Everywhere and in everything he saw "enemies," "two-facers" and "spies." Possessing unlimited power, he indulged in great willfulness and choked a person morally and physically. A situation was created where one could not express one's own will. When Stalin said that one or another would be arrested, it was necessary to accept on faith that he was an "enemy of the people." What proofs were offered? The confession of the arrested.... How is it possible that a person confesses to crimes that he had not committed? Only in one way—because of application of physical methods of pressuring him, tortures...taking away his human dignity....

Troubles in Poland

The effects of Khrushchev's speech spread quickly. In China the ruling Communist party, led by Mao Zedong, was disturbed. The Chinese accepted Stalin's ideas on communism, and they had used many of his methods for gaining total control. Partly because of Khrushchev's secret speech, they began to challenge the Soviet Union's role as the leader of world communism. In Eastern Europe some ruling Communists worried what would happen in their countries. Under Khrushchev the Soviet Union's more liberal positions might encourage some Eastern Europeans to seek changes—changes that would threaten the power of their Communist leaders.

In Poland the call for political change came just a few months after Khrushchev's speech. In late June workers in the industrial city of Poznan went on strike. They demanded better working conditions and more freedom. The government responded by sending in hundreds of tanks and thousands of soldiers. In the clashes that followed, nearly 50 workers died.

Some members of the Polish Communist party now talked about trying to reform their government. These reformers wanted to bring Wladyslaw Gomulka, a former Communist leader, back into power. Gomulka was considered a nationalist—someone who might support Poland's interests over the interests of the Soviet Union. Under Stalin's orders Gomulka had been kicked out of the party in 1948 and placed under arrest. He had been freed from prison just two months before the June 1956 strikes.

Khrushchev had mixed feelings about Gomulka, but he decided that Gomulka would be better than the existing Polish leader, Edward Ochab. The Communists put Gomulka in charge. Then, in October 1956 Gomulka and the Polish Communists angered Khrushchev. They planned to remove a Soviet officer,

Marshal Konstantin Rokossvsky, from his leadership post in the Polish Communist party. Khrushchev flew to Warsaw to confront Gomulka, and Soviet troops stationed in Poland slowly advanced toward the capital.

In the United States, President Eisenhower said, "Our hearts go out" to the Poles, but once again he was not going to get directly involved. Secretary of State Dulles said it would not be "profitable or desirable" for U.S. troops to go into Poland. "It would be the last thing in the world that these people who are trying to win their independence would want. That would precipitate a full-scale war and probably the result of that would be all these people wiped out."

During his meeting with Gomulka, Khrushchev threatened to use force to assert Soviet control over Poland. Gomulka replied that he had the firm support of the Polish army and the people. Khrushchev finally agreed to accept the removal of Rokossvsky. In return Gomulka promised that Poland would remain loyal to the Soviet Union, which was Khrushchev's real concern. By October 24 the crisis was largely over. But a new crisis was just starting in another Soviet satellite.

Sources   POLAND IN 1956

Polish workers strike during the June 1956 Poznan protests.

Flora Lewis was a journalist for the *New York Times* in Poland at the time of the 1956 crisis. Here are some of her observations of the time.

You could sense that there was resistance. So that when the uprising broke out in Poznan…it was not a terrible surprise; there had been mounting tensions. And that uprising then had a tremendous impact in forcing open the situation in the whole country, which led very much to what happened in October '56....

What really shocked the government, the regime, was that it was the workers who rose, it was not the people that they were afraid of. It was not the...intellectuals; it was not people involved in politics. It was real workers and they were disgusted. So that was a terrible blow to the regime.

...[C]ulturally, American films got more and more banned and Soviet films had to be showed, and [the] Soviet-Polish friendship society took over all the entertainments, and the press was very much controlled, what could be said, the public books. So there was a heavy hand....

Rise of a Revolution

The events in Poland stirred feelings of sympathy in Hungary. On October 23, 1956, Hungarian students began to demonstrate in Budapest, the capital. They called for free speech, the elimination of the Hungarian secret police, and the withdrawal of Soviet troops. The secret police fired at the crowd. But the police action did not stop the protesters. Workers joined the students, and together they toppled a giant statue of Stalin in the center of Budapest.

Hungarian Uprising #2

Erno Gero, the leader of the Hungarian Communist party, sent a message to Moscow asking for Soviet troops to step in. On the morning of October 24, 30,000 heavily armed Soviet soldiers, along with tanks, entered Budapest. The protesters refused to back down, and the Soviet troops opened fire. Over the next several days, hundreds of Hungarians died in the assault. They fought back with rifles and homemade bombs called "Molotov cocktails."

Imre Nagy, the new premier of Hungary, appealed to the rebels for an end to the protests. Nagy was a moderate who had been removed from power the year before. Soviet leaders returned him to power as the rebellion began, hoping he could end the revolt. But

Hungarians jam the streets of Budapest in 1956, protesting communism.

Nagy did not realize how strongly the Hungarians felt about challenging communism.

Gurgely Pongracz was one of the Hungarians in the streets. He said, "It wasn't the Soviet Union or the Russian people we were against. We were against the system, the Communist system. A lot of Russian soldiers, they were sympathizing with us during the revolution.... In fact we had quite a few who died [fighting] on our side." Hungarian troops also deserted their government to fight with the rebels.

Nagy told his people that once order was restored, all Soviet troops would leave. He promised to talk with Moscow about permanently removing Soviet forces from Hungary. The Soviet leaders debated how to handle the situation. For a brief time, they decided to support Nagy and withdraw troops from Budapest. But the Soviet Union also prepared to send more troops to the Hungarian border, ready to attack if the rebels stirred again.

People   IMRE NAGY

During Imre Nagy's last years in Hungary, his political career took a series of twists and turns. After World War II, he served in the Hungarian government until he spoke out against certain policies and was forced out of office.

Nagy was born on June 7, 1896, in Kaposvar, Hungary. During World War I,

he fought for the Austro-Hungarian Empire and was captured by the Russian army. After the Russian Revolution of 1917, Nagy joined the Bolshevik party and became a Soviet citizen. He returned to Hungary just after World War I and took a position there in a new Communist government. When that government collapsed, Nagy worked secretly to organize a new Communist party. He was arrested in 1927, but he managed to escape and return to the Soviet Union. He stayed there until 1944.

Nagy returned to Budapest at the end of World War II, when Soviet troops were occupying the city. His political career reached its peak in June 1953, when he was named premier, but two years later he was out of office. During the October 1956 uprising, Nagy was put back into power by the Soviet Union. He tried to reform the government while negotiating a Soviet withdrawal. He felt betrayed when the Soviet military refused to withdraw completely from Hungary. He then took the bold step of proclaiming Hungarian neutrality. This move was quickly reversed by the invading Soviet troops.

After Nagy was captured by Soviet forces, he was held prisoner for almost two years. After refusing to support the new Communist government in Hungary, he was executed on June 16, 1958.

The End of Freedom

A cease-fire was arranged for October 28. Both sides had suffered hundreds of casualties in the fighting. The Soviet troops pulled out of Budapest, and the backers of the rebellion demanded changes. Workers took over buildings and formed their own councils. Some people had the sense that Hungary had won its freedom in the revolution. British journalist Charles Wheeler said, "People were enormously optimistic that life had changed. Everywhere in the country the Hungarian [flag] was flying with the...Communist emblem torn out. It was, seemed to be, a completely liberated country."

Hungarians working for Radio Free Europe claimed in their broadcasts that the West supported the rebels and their push for freedom. In theory this was true. But once again, as in Poland, the United States had no plans to use its armed forces to help the Hungarians. U.S. State Department official Robert Bowie said, "The policy...was don't...create any hope on the part of the satellite countries that we will intervene." The Hungarians soon learned for themselves the limits of American support.

After the October 28 cease-fire, Nagy made plans to create a more democratic government. Other parties besides the Communist party would be allowed to enter politics. Soviet leaders had initially supported Nagy and some of his proposed changes, but now they began to waver. Khrushchev felt pressure to act. Said his son, Sergei, "It was a very complicated decision for my father as he thought for three or four days.... We have to use force? Yes? No? Yes? No? At last it was [his] decision, yes to use it."

On November 1, the day after Khrushchev made this decision, Nagy declared that Hungary was withdrawing from the Warsaw Pact and becoming a neutral state like neighboring Austria. Two days later, tens of thousands of Soviet troops and more than 4,000 tanks rolled toward Budapest. They entered the city the next morning. Soviet leaders wanted to preserve communism in Hungary under their control. "We were not a force of occupation," claimed Soviet major Grigori Dobrynov. "Instead we were going in as saviors to protect the people from banditry and terrorism."

The rebels took to the streets with whatever weapons they could find. Many Hungarian soldiers fought by their sides. During the fighting the rebels broadcast a plea for help: "Civilized people of the world: on the watch tower of 1,000-year-old Hungary, the last flames begin to go out. The Soviet army is attempting to crush our troubled hearts. Listen to our call. Help us... with action, with soldiers

Thousands of Soviet tanks such as this one helped to crush the Hungarian uprising.

and arms. Our ship is sinking. The light vanishes. The shadows grow darker...."

But no help came. Leaders in the United States and Western Europe were focused on a new crisis in Egypt, over the Suez Canal. Soviet troops moved into Hungary while the West's attention was on Egypt. The Soviet troops eventually crushed the outgunned Hungarians. Almost 20,000 people were killed or wounded—most of them Hungarian.

After briefly going into hiding, Nagy was taken prisoner by Soviet troops. He was deceived into believing that he would be allowed to go to Yugoslavia. Meanwhile, a new Communist government—one loyal to Moscow—was installed. About 200,000 Hungarians fled to Austria before the Soviet Union closed the border. The other Eastern European countries had learned a lesson: Do not stray far from Soviet wishes. They also realized that the United States had little power to influence events behind the "iron curtain" without risking war.

Sources NAGY'S LAST SPEECH

As Soviet troops stormed Budapest, Imre Nagy made one last radio broadcast to the Hungarian people—and the world. Here is an excerpt from that speech.

This fight is the fight for freedom by the Hungarian people against the Russian intervention, and it is possible that I shall only be able to stay at my post for one or two hours. The whole world will see how the Russian armed forces, contrary to all treaties and conventions, are crushing the resistance of the Hungarian people. They will also see how they are kidnapping the prime minister of a country which is a member of the United Nations...and therefore it cannot be doubted at all that this is the most brutal form of intervention.... The leaders [of the revolution] should turn to all the people of the world for help and explain that today it is Hungary and tomorrow, or the day after tomorrow, it will be the turn of other countries, because the imperialism of Moscow does not know borders and is only trying to play for time.

Egypt's Suez Canal links the Mediterranean and Red Seas. Opened in 1869, the 101-mile (162-km) canal cuts the ocean trip from London to India by 5,000 miles (8,046 km). The canal was financed mostly by French investors, though all of Europe—and particularly Great Britain—relied on this waterway. By 1875 Britain owned a controlling interest in the Suez Canal, and it later sent troops to Egypt to protect the canal and other British investments there.

Politics within Egypt, and the Cold War outside it, affected developments at the Suez Canal. In 1952 General Gamal Abdel Nasser was one of a group of officers who took over the Egyptian government. By 1954 Nasser was in complete control. He wanted to end British influence in Egypt. Nasser also turned to the Soviet Union and Communist China to buy weapons. This upset U.S. leaders, and in May 1956 they canceled plans to help Egypt build a new dam. In response Nasser seized control of the Suez Canal, which was still owned by the British. He planned to use the tolls collected from ships on the canal to pay for the dam.

At this time Egypt was also involved in a long-standing conflict with Israel. In the late summer and early fall of 1956 the Israelis, together with the French and British, planned an attack on Egypt. Israel struck first. Then on October 31, 1956, British and French forces moved in to take control of the canal. The attack angered President Eisenhower, who had not been informed of the plan. He tried to end the fighting through the UN. The attack also took world attention away from the events in Hungary, especially after Khrushchev threatened to widen the Suez war by attacking French and British forces.

France and Britain soon withdrew their troops, and the Suez Canal remained under Egyptian control. Eisenhower sent a letter to former British prime minister Winston Churchill, expressing his displeasure about the attack on Egypt. "The Soviets," Eisenhower wrote, "are the real enemy and all else must be viewed against the background of that truth."

4

INTO SPACE

The Cold War and the resulting arms race led both the Soviet Union and the United States to improve old technologies and develop new ones. In 1955 the United States *deployed* a new long-range bomber, the B-52. The plane was designed to cover up to 8,800 miles (14,160 km) without refueling. With this range it could fly deep into Soviet territory and drop nuclear bombs.

The next year the Soviet military introduced its own long-range bomber, the Tu-95 Bear. The Bear was also capable of carrying nuclear bombs. At the Moscow Air Show, ten of the planes were displayed. Said Georgi Mikhailov, a Soviet general, "For the Americans, seeing ten planes capable of reaching the United States was a shock. At that time...they supposed that the Soviet Union didn't have any means of delivery to the United States."

Soviet Tu-95 Bear bombers streak through the sky.

A new fear grew in the United States about a so-called "bomber gap" between America and the Soviet Union. Herbert York, a nuclear physicist working for the U.S. government, said, "We took it seriously...the idea that there was going to be a bomber gap, that somehow we were coming to a period of time when the Russians would have even more bombers than we did, at least more intercontinental bombers...." The idea of a bomber gap led President Eisenhower to double the number of B-52s produced.

The B-52 was built to replace the bomber planes flown during World War II and the Korean War. Airplane-maker Boeing first produced the B-52A in 1954 and the B-52B the next year. The last version of the plane, the B-52H, was produced in 1962. More than 700 B-52s were built during those years. The B-52 is a type of warplane known as a heavy bomber. Some crew members called the plane "Buff," for "Big, Ugly, Fat Fellow."

Equipped with eight large jet engines, the B-52 was designed to carry nuclear bombs for up to 8,800 miles (14,160 km). In its first years of service, some of the planes remained in the air at all times, carrying nuclear bombs. With this tactic the U.S. Air Force could prevent a possible surprise attack against all of the planes while they were on the ground.

During the Vietnam War, the U.S. military used B-52s to drop *conventional* (non-nuclear) *weapons*. One B-52 could carry up to 35 tons of bombs on a mission. Today, the air force can use the B-52 to drop conventional bombs and to fire cruise missiles. These guided missiles can hit targets at sea or on land, and they can carry either nuclear or conventional warheads. The bomber can also patrol over the world's oceans to detect the movement of enemy ships. If necessary the B-52 could still be used to carry nuclear bombs.

The B-52 has flown for the U.S. military since the 1950s.

Searching for the Bomber Gap

United States officials wanted a better idea of how many bombers the Soviet Union had. They also wanted to keep track of any new weapons the Soviet military developed. In the late 1940s and early 1950s, SAC flew reconfigured bombers into Soviet airspace on *reconnaissance* missions. At least a few of these planes were shot down by Soviet air defense units. The incidents were usually kept quiet, but there was always a danger that events could escalate. These flights to gather information were authorized by President Harry Truman, but in the spring of 1950, he temporarily suspended the flights after a modified B-29 was shot down.

By 1956 the U.S. government was once again ready to fly reconnaissance missions over the Soviet Union. The air force now had a plane designed just for that purpose—the U-2. This spy plane could fly at 75,000 feet (22,860 m)—about five miles (8 km) higher than the best Soviet fighter plane of the era could fly. The U-2 also flew out of the range of Soviet *antiaircraft* guns. It was supposed to cruise over the Soviet Union and gather information without being seen or stopped.

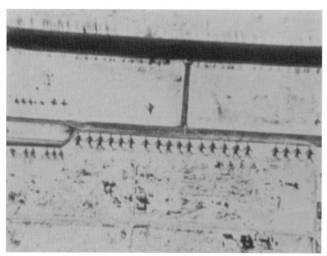

The U-2 used a sophisticated camera to photograph the area below it. A picture taken from the plane's highest altitude could clearly capture a newspaper headline being read on the ground.

This photo, taken from a U-2 spy plane, shows jets lined up at a Soviet airfield.

The U-2's spy missions were dangerous. Nuclear physicist Herbert York said, "Everyone knew that the U-2 was a deliberate violation of international norms and everyone knew that eventually...it would be shot down, but nevertheless the need for better information than we had, the perception of the need was so great that we went ahead anyway."

Marty Knutson was one of the first U-2 pilots. On one of his missions, he photographed an airfield filled with Tu-95 bombers. Knutson later said, "I knew right then...that this had to be the most important picture ever taken by a reconnaissance pilot." Knutson was convinced that his photo proved the bomber gap existed. Only later did U.S. leaders learn that Knutson had photographed the entire Soviet long-range bomber fleet. There was no bomber gap. But going into 1957, American fears turned to a new Soviet offensive weapon.

Espionage — EYES IN THE SKY

Both the United States and the Soviet Union relied on spies to gather information. But tools like the U-2 spy plane helped provide data that human agents could not uncover. The U-2 was the world's first plane built just for spying, and its flights were controlled by the CIA.

The U-2 carried only the pilot and a camera that weighed about 500 pounds (227 kg). The idea for putting a high-quality camera in a high-flying plane came from Edwin Land, the developer of the Polaroid instant camera. Land

U-2 in flight

was one of the people who convinced President Eisenhower to build the U-2.

The U-2 was designed and flown in great secrecy. It was a difficult plane to build because it had to be lightweight, fly at high altitudes, and cover thousands of miles without refueling. Built by Lockheed Aircraft, the finished product had long, thin wings, almost like a glider plane. The wings also carried most of the plane's fuel. For many years the U-2 held the record for highest altitude flown by a plane.

The role of the U-2 was eventually reduced by spy *satellites* and another spy plane, the SR-71A Blackbird. But the U.S. Air Force still flies a newer model of the U-2. This plane was used for reconnaissance during the 1991 Gulf War against Iraq.

The Missile Era Begins

As U.S. leaders worried about a bomber gap, they and Soviet leaders were already planning for a new way to deliver nuclear weapons. Since the end of World War II, both countries had been working on rocket technology. Much of the work was done by German scientists who had developed rockets for Nazi leader Adolf Hitler. These scientists now worked for either the Americans or the Russians. Rockets could carry explosive devices over long distances with great accuracy. By the early 1950s, the Americans and Russians realized rocket technology could propel huge missiles that carried nuclear weapons.

Oleg Troyanovski, an advisor to Nikita Khrushchev, said, "Khrushchev...came to the conclusion that missiles were the weapons of the future, and that warships were getting obsolete, bombers were getting obsolete. That we should concentrate everything on missiles."

Soviet scientists worked on their missile program in a remote desert in the republic of Kazakhstan. Said one technician on the project, "We were kept in such strict secrecy that we couldn't mention the word 'missile' even between ourselves. It was called 'the mechanism,' 'the product.'" The weapon the scientists worked on would be able to strike the United States from the Soviet Union—it would be an *intercontinental ballistic missile* (ICBM).

The United States was also developing an ICBM. Working for the Americans was Wernher von Braun, a German scientist who had moved to the United States after World War II. In 1956 von Braun designed a rocket capable of traveling from one continent to another. However, his project was outside of the official government missile program. In May 1957 the Soviet Union tested the first ICBM, winning that stage of the arms race. But the greater shock to Americans came a few months later with the launch of a small metal object called *Sputnik*.

Sputnik in Space

In the fall of 1957, Soviet leaders talked about placing a satellite into orbit around Earth. Some Americans considered this mere 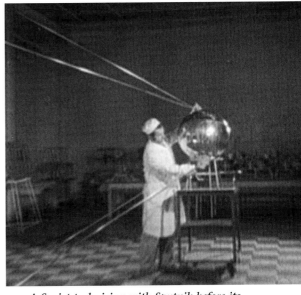 Sputnik #3 propaganda. The launch of a Soviet rocket early in the morning on October 5, 1957, showed that the Russians were serious. Inside the rocket was a satellite called *Sputnik*—Russian for "companion." Khrushchev, when he heard the news, said, "Frankly, I never thought it would work," and went back to bed. The reaction to *Sputnik* was more dramatic in the United States.

By launching a satellite into space, the Soviet Union proved it could also launch a rocket carrying nuclear warheads. The United States now faced the threat of a direct nuclear attack with little advance warning. One Soviet air force general had already declared,

A Soviet technician with Sputnik before its historic flight into space.

What was inaccessible before has now become quite accessible. The modern means of air attack which have tremendous speeds and can operate over vast distances, are capable of striking at any point of the globe. The means of conveyance for hydrogen bombs...make it possible to bring them instantly to the remotest areas of any continent of the world....

Sputnik was also a blow to American pride, since the Soviet Union had been first to launch a satellite. The United States had been working on satellites for scientific exploration. In addition, the U.S. military was secretly building reconnaissance satellites. Andrew Goodpaster, an aide to President Eisenhower, said *Sputnik* "had given our people quite a jolt, almost of panic proportions to think that the Soviets could do that...." Scientist Edward Teller told the country that the United States had lost "a battle more important and greater than Pearl Harbor."

President Eisenhower tried to calm the furor over *Sputnik*. "Our satellite program," he said, "has never been conducted as a race with other nations.... I consider our country's satellite program to be well designed and properly scheduled to achieve the scientific purpose for which it was initiated."

Away from the public, however, Eisenhower and his aides worried about the reaction to *Sputnik* around the world. Notes from a meeting of the NSC recorded their concerns that America's best allies "require assurance that we have not been passed scientifically and militarily by the USSR." Some council members suggested that the United States needed to take a bold step to achieve its own firsts in the new space race. Eisenhower did not agree. He believed it was impossible for the country to try to surpass the Soviet Union in every scientific program. Instead, the U.S. goal, he said, should be to "seek a military posture that the Russians will respect."

While the Soviet Union and the United States were building bombs and ICBMs, some people in the West were speaking out against the nuclear arms race. One group in the United States was the National Committee for a Sane Nuclear Policy, known as SANE. The month after the *Sputnik* launch, SANE published a statement in the *New York Times* protesting nuclear weapons. Here is part of that statement.

We are facing a danger unlike any danger that has ever existed. In our possession and in the possession of the Russians are more than enough nuclear explosives to put an end to the life of man on earth....

Just in front of us opens a grand human adventure into outer space. But within us and all around us is the need to make this world whole before we set out for other ones. We can earn the right to explore other planets only as we make this one safe and fit for human habitation....

...[T]he test of a nation's right to survive today is measured not by the size of its bombs or the range of its missiles, but by the size and range of its concerns for the human community as a whole.

There can be no true security for America unless we can exert leadership in these terms, unless we become advocates of a grand design that is directed to the large cause of human destiny.

Technology SPUTNIK

Sputnik was a silver metal ball with thin rods trailing behind it. It measured 22 inches (56 cm) wide—about twice the size of a basketball. *Sputnik* was the first object made by humans to orbit Earth, and it stirred great fears in the United States. Now, it seemed, Soviet scientists could surpass the efforts of the best minds in the United States.

Sputnik was launched in October 1957. Inside it was a tiny radio transmitter. When the satellite reached its orbit, about 500 miles (800 km) above Earth, the radio began sending a signal. Some people compared the sound to that of a chirping cricket. *Sputnik* circled the planet once every 96 minutes until early 1958. Then it fell back toward Earth and burned up in the atmosphere.

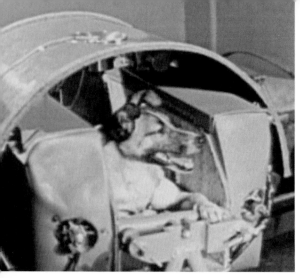

Laika, the canine cosmonaut, prepares for her journey into space.

A month after the launch of *Sputnik*, the Soviet Union sent up a second satellite, *Sputnik II*. This time the satellite carried a passenger—a small dog named Laika. She became the first animal in space. Laika lived for ten days inside *Sputnik II*, showing that it was possible for living creatures to survive in space. It would be only a few years before humans also orbited Earth.

Sources ☭ COMMENTS ON SPUTNIK

In the days after the launch of *Sputnik*, officials from both the Soviet Union and the United States had plenty to say. Here are selections from an article published on October 9, 1957, in *Pravda*, the official newspaper of the Soviet Communist party.

The prominent scientists of today are speaking of the arrival of a new era, of that period in the history of civilization when a gigantic step forward has been made in the conquest of interplanetary space. Herein lies the historic significance of the Soviet discovery.

Today the entire population of the Earth sees the great victory of our Soviet science and technology, our highly developed industry, our technical might, which the great Soviet people created under the leadership of the Communist Party.... This is a victory of collective labor, which alone is capable of creating real wonders in the world.

Here are comments made by U.S. Secretary of State John Foster Dulles about *Sputnik* at a news conference.

I feel absolutely confident that there is no doubt whatsoever of our ability to move ahead and, I believe, keep ahead in [the missile] field. As I said before, I think that perhaps it is a good thing that this satellite was put up in good time, so that there would not be an undue complacency anywhere. I do not think that there has been complacency within the [Eisenhower] administration, but there has been a certain complacency, I think, felt generally that we were almost ahead of the Russians in every aspect. Well, that is not so, and those of us who have been close to the situation have, I think, realized that for some time. You cannot take a nation the size of the Soviet Union, under the kind of despotic government they have, and have it concentrate for now forty years upon almost a single objective without getting some results....

I think [Sputnik] has created a unity of purpose and thinking between the administration, the Congress, and the people which is very desirable at this stage.

Failure and Finally Success

After *Sputnik* President Eisenhower felt growing pressure to launch a U.S. satellite as fast as possible. A satellite was already scheduled for launch in early 1958, but the date was moved up to December 6, 1957. A navy rocket under development, called Vanguard, was supposed to carry a four-pound (1.8-kg) satellite into space.

At the launch, journalists and public officials gathered to watch the historic moment. The Vanguard rose just a few feet off the ground, then exploded. According to Herbert York, the failure

A Vanguard rocket carrying the first U.S. satellite bursts into flames.

of this launch embarrassed the United States "because it was accompanied by a lot of fanfare and a lot of boasting about what our intentions were. Eisenhower eventually became very sensitive on that point...."

Eisenhower had other troubles, as well. His Democratic opponents in Congress began complaining about a "missile gap" with the Soviet Union. They learned about a secret government study, the Gaither Report, that talked about the Russians' growing technological power. Eisenhower did not want to release the report, but its findings were eventually published in the *Washington Post*.

York was one of the authors of this report. At the time he and the other people involved with it thought they had done a good job. York later changed his judgment: "But there was very little real expertise with respect to the question of either what the Russians are doing or what the American response should be.... Eisenhower's [judgment] that it was an overreaction, I think, was right...."

Eisenhower believed the United States was already spending enough money and taking the right actions for its military defense. He also had growing evidence that there was no missile gap. The Soviet Union actually had only a few ICBMs. Additionally the United States had many more nuclear warheads than the Soviet military did. But Eisenhower could not reveal this information, since it came from the still-secret U-2 spy plane program.

Eisenhower and the American public finally got some good news in January 1958. The first U.S. satellite, *Explorer*, reached orbit. It was powered into space by a rocket developed by Wernher von Braun. When Eisenhower heard the news, he said, "I sure feel a lot better now."

Trying to Catch Up

Although glad about the success of *Explorer*, many Americans thought the United States still had work to do. If the country trailed the Soviet Union in the space race, then perhaps American education had to improve. Some people thought America needed more scientists and engineers, as well as a government program devoted to space exploration. In 1958 Congress and Eisenhower tried to fill those perceived needs.

In July the government created the *National Aeronautics and Space Administration* (NASA). This new administration received money from the military's missile program to begin work on rockets for space exploration. NASA was also put in charge of developing a spy satellite to replace the U-2. In addition, Eisenhower approved more money for the defense budget, one of the recommendations of the Gaither Report.

Two months later Congress passed the National Defense Education Act. The bill gave federal money to help schools create new programs in science, mathematics, and foreign languages—including Russian. Money was also set aside for loans to college students studying math and science. According to one university professor, higher education was now "as essential...as supersonic bombers" for America's defense.

Some Americans at this time were reluctant to spend more on defense and increase the possibility of confrontation with the Soviet Union. George Kennan was one of them. At the beginning of the Cold War, Kennan had helped shape the U.S. policy of containment. Now, he talked about *disengagement* in Europe and a return to diplomacy. Kennan said that all foreign troops should disengage (pull out) from East and West Germany and Eastern Europe. He also called for reducing America's reliance on nuclear weapons. Kennan said, "A defense posture built around a weapon suicidal in its implications can serve in the long run only to paralyze national policy...and to drive everyone deeper and deeper into the hopeless exertions of the weapons race."

But most Americans still believed the Soviet Union was the enemy in a war of *ideology*. They also felt that the Cold War of words and ideas could become a real war with nuclear weapons. As a child in the 1950s, Jean Asam lived in New Jersey. She remembered the message she learned in school and through the media: "It was...the Americans versus the Russians back then and they were...the bad people that would come and take over our lifestyle...and...somehow you needed to be able to protect yourself."

The Bomb SHELTER FROM THE NUCLEAR STORM

As fears of a Soviet nuclear attack grew, the United States increased its civil defense programs. More air-raid shelters were built, and students continued to practice their duck-and-cover tactics. Some Americans even built their own private bomb shelters for extra protection from a Soviet attack.

An American tests a backyard bomb shelter.

Companies advertised shelters that could support a family of five for weeks at a time. The shelters came with canned food and water. The U.S. government also published books showing people how to build their own shelters in their basements. Illustrations showed small rooms with brick or cement walls eight to ten inches (20.3 to 25.4 cm) thick.

A few years later, in 1961 the magazine *Life* devoted an entire issue to surviving nuclear fallout. In the magazine John F. Kennedy, then the president of the United States, urged Americans to "prepare for all eventualities. The ability to survive coupled with the will to do so...are essential to our country."

5

GOOD TIMES AND BAD

Even as the Cold War went on and the space race gathered steam, the United States and the Soviet Union kept talking, trying to keep civil relations. In October 1958 representatives from America, Great Britain, and the Soviet Union met in Geneva, Switzerland, to talk about limiting nuclear weapons testing. (Great Britain had tested its first nuclear bomb in 1952.) The interest in limiting these tests had been growing since the mid-1950s. Earlier in 1958 an international group of scientists had met in Geneva and agreed on ways to monitor nuclear tests. However, the October meeting ended with no agreement to ban further tests.

A diplomatic event that was not tied to the arms race occurred in the summer of 1959. The United States took part in a cultural and trade fair in Moscow. This fair was a sign of the on-going attempt to have normal relations in the middle of the Cold War. It was also another sign of Khrushchev's desire to open up his country to the West. But even this innocent display of American commerce led to some tension.

Vice President Richard Nixon helped open the American National Exhibition at the trade fair. Nixon was the highest-ranking U.S. official to visit Moscow since the start of the Cold War. He and Khrushchev ended up at a part of the exhibit that featured the products of a modern American kitchen. The two men exchanged words about the merits of the American economic system versus the Soviet system. The discussion had actually started earlier in the day, and parts of it were broadcast on television. The Nixon-Khrushchev exchange was later called the "kitchen debate." The two men tried to keep calm, but their words showed the intense differences between the Cold War rivals.

Nikita Khrushchev and Richard Nixon meet during the "kitchen debate."

Here are some excerpts from the July 1959 debate between Richard Nixon and Nikita Khrushchev. The first came as the men looked at new color television technology.

Nixon: *There are some instances where you may be ahead of us. For example in the development of the thrust of your rockets for the investigation of outer space. There may be some instances for example, color television, where we're ahead of you. But in order for both of us...*

Khrushchev: *No, we are up with you on this, too. We have bested you in one technology and also in the other.*

Nixon: *You see, you never concede anything.*

Khrushchev: *I do not give up.*

The second exchange took place in a model kitchen.

Nixon: *This is the newest model. This is the kind which is built in thousands of units for direct installation in the houses.... Our steel workers, as you know, are on strike. But any steelworker could buy this house. They earn $3 an hour. This house costs about $100 a month to buy on a contract running 25 to 30 years....*

Khrushchev: *The Americans have created their own image of the Soviet man and thinks he is as you want him to be. But he is not as you think. You think the Russian people will be dumbfounded to see these things, but the fact is that newly built Russian houses have all this equipment right now. Moreover, all you have to do to get a house is to be born in the Soviet Union.... Yet you say that we are slaves to communism.*

Khrushchev Comes to America

An official diplomatic meeting between the United States and the Soviet Union was held in Geneva in 1959. France and Great Britain also attended. The meeting did not lead to any new agreements, but it did create an atmosphere that led to Khrushchev's visiting the United States. Some Americans questioned Eisenhower's decision to invite Khrushchev. The president assured his critics that the invitation "implied no hint of a surrender."

Arriving on a Soviet Tu-144, the world's largest airplane at the time, Khrushchev landed in New York City on September 15. He traveled across America, stopping at a Pittsburgh steel mill and meeting film stars in Hollywood. In Iowa the Soviet leader visited a farm and tried his first hot dog. Khrushchev spent his last few days with Eisenhower at the presidential retreat, Camp David, in Maryland.

The two men got along well. Khrushchev's son, Sergei, said, "When they [spoke] as human beings, [people] who went through the two wars, their understanding with each other was very good.... But when they sat [at] the table of the negotiations, they could not solve any problems. But in reality, they really built the foundations of future peace relations."

Khrushchev tried to soften one of his earlier statements, a threat that the Soviet Union would "bury" *capitalism*. Instead, he insisted that Americans could "live under capitalism and we will live under socialism and build communism. The one whose system proves better will win." He also assured Eisenhower that the Soviet Union did not want war.

Khrushchev left the meetings in a good mood. He and others referred later to the "spirit of Camp David" that might lead to better relations. Eisenhower did not share the same enthusiasm about this spirit, but he did agree to meet in Paris with Khrushchev and

President Dwight D. Eisenhower welcomes Khrushchev to Camp David, Maryland.

leaders from Britain and

France the next spring. Eisenhower also made plans to visit the Soviet Union. New events changed both of those plans.

The U-2 Mess

The United States had been continuing to send the U-2 on spy missions over the Soviet Union. The plane provided valuable information about the Soviet military. On May 1, 1960, just two weeks before the Paris meeting, a U-2 left Pakistan for a flight over the Soviet Union. Its pilot, Francis Gary Powers, was looking for new Soviet antiaircraft defenses. He found them—in a most unfortunate way.

When Soviet radar first picked up the U-2, fighter planes were sent after it. When the fighters failed to stop the U-2, the Russians fired a new missile, the S-5. The missile sent the U-2 crashing to the ground, and Powers ejected from the plane. When he landed near the city of Sverdlosk, he was captured and taken prisoner.

The United States had created a story to cover up any U-2 spy mission that failed. The U-2 was simply a high-altitude weather plane. A State Department official offered this explanation of Powers and his plane: "It is entirely possible that having a failure in the oxygen equipment…could result in the pilot losing consciousness, [and] the plane continued on automatic pilot for some considerable distance, and accidentally violated Soviet air space."

But Khrushchev did not accept the U.S. response. He knew the U-2 was on a spy mission, and he had both the wrecked plane and the pilot as evidence. Said Soviet advisor Oleg Troyanovski, "Khrushchev gathered us around him and said, 'Look, we are going to take a very tough position because otherwise our public simply will not understand. We'll have to make a statement saying the president should apologize, should punish those responsible for these flights, and should say that they will not be repeated any longer.'"

Khrushchev displays photos taken from Francis Gary Powers's downed U-2 spy plane.

Eisenhower did finally admit that the U-2 was on a spy mission. But he refused to apologize or guarantee that the United States would stop its spy flights. Khrushchev, who was already in Paris for the planned summit meeting, angrily returned to Moscow. The summit never happened. Eisenhower called the incident "the stupid U-2 mess." But his term as president was almost over. He had no more Cold War messes to handle.

Technology   THE CORONA SATELLITE

While Francis Gary Powers was flying his last U-2 mission, the United States was already working on a new way to take pictures over the Soviet Union. A spy satellite called *Corona* would circle Earth and take pictures of the Soviet Union from space. To hide its spy mission, the government called *Corona* a scientific research satellite.

Corona, the world's first photo reconnaissance satellite, began taking pictures on August 18, 1960. From an altitude of more than 100 miles (160 km),

Corona's camera could cover an area about 10 miles (16 km) wide by 120 miles (192 km) long. The film was then automatically placed in cans that were ejected from the satellite and parachuted to Earth. From 1960 until 1972, more than 100 different satellites were used for spying, taking more than 800,000 pictures from space. The *Corona* mission was classified, or kept secret, until 1995. Now, images taken from the satellite are available for public viewing.

The items found on Powers when he was captured.

Throughout the Cold War, spies on both sides carried special tools designed for defense or for assassination. When Francis Gary Powers crashed, the things he carried convinced his Soviet captors that he was a spy. He had a poison needle, which he could use to commit suicide if he feared being tortured. He also carried a silenced gun.

Methods of silencing guns had been developed during World War II. A silencer fits onto the barrel of a gun. It both muffles the sound of the bullet and reduces the flash created when a bullet leaves the gun. Silenced guns also use special bullets that travel at slow speeds. This helps reduce the sound of the gun blast.

Suicide poisons were designed to prevent spies from revealing important information to their captors under torture. These fast-acting poisons come as pills, liquids, or coatings on the tips of needles. One drop of the poison on the needle is strong enough to kill a person. Powers's needle was hidden inside a silver dollar.

In the early 1950s, the Soviet Union developed a gun that looked like a cigarette case. Fake cigarettes inside the case fired bullets filled with poison. Tiny knives were also useful for cutting ropes or attacking enemies at close range. One of these spy knives featured a curved blade attached to the back of a coin.

In April 1956 Francis Gary Powers resigned as a pilot with the U.S. Air Force to take a job with the CIA. He was a civilian, but his new flying career was more dangerous than anything he had faced in the military. Powers was one of a handful of pilots chosen to fly a U-2 spy plane.

Born on August 17, 1929, in Burdine, Kentucky, Powers enlisted in the air force during the Korean War but never saw combat. After joining the CIA, Powers flew the U-2 on spy missions along the Soviet border. Late in 1956 he made his first flight over the Soviet Union.

During his flight of May 1, 1960, Powers had been in the air for four hours when he heard a dull thump outside the plane. He later wrote that "the aircraft jerked forward, and a tremendous orange flash lit the cockpit and the sky.... [A] violent movement shook the plane, flinging me all over the cockpit....

What was left of the plane began spinning, only upside down, the nose spinning upward toward the sky, the tail down toward the ground. All I could see was blue sky, spinning, spinning."

After his capture by the Soviet Union, Powers went on trial as a spy. Soviet officials displayed his espionage tools as evidence. He was convicted and given a ten-year sentence. In 1962 the United States swapped captured Soviet spy Rudolf Abel for Powers. He returned to the United States and worked as a test pilot and helicopter pilot. Powers died in a helicopter crash on August 1, 1977.

Sources TWO VIEWS OF THE U-2 AFFAIR

The first selection here includes excerpts from a memo sent to the State Department by officials at the U.S. embassy in Moscow. The document reflects growing concern over the handling of the U-2 crisis.

There is no doubt that we have suffered major loss in Soviet public opinion and probably throughout the world....

Judging by display which Khrushchev made of evidence...I would doubt that we can continue to deny charges of deliberate overflight.... I should recommend [Eisenhower deny he knew of the flight]. I would suggest this might also be accompanied by statement that espionage practiced on both sides and most successfully by Soviet Union which can exploit openness [of] our society.

...If we have available any provable evidence of comparable Soviet actions these might be mentioned but I believe only if they are adequate.

The second selection is from a Soviet note sent to the United States more than a week after the plane was shot down.

Upon examination by experts of all data at the disposal of the Soviet side, it was incontrovertibly established that the intruder aircraft belonged to the United States of America, was permanently based in Turkey and was sent through Pakistan into the Soviet Union with hostile purposes....

...This aircraft was specially equipped for reconnaissance...over the territory of the Soviet Union. It had on board apparatus for aerial photography for detecting the Soviet radar network and other special radio-technical equipment which form part of U.S.S.R. anti-aircraft defenses....

One must ask, how is it possible to reconcile this with declarations on the part of leading figures of the United States of America that the Government of the United States of America...strives for improvement of relations between the Union of Soviet Socialist Republics and...America, for relaxation of international tension, and strengthening of trust between states. Military intelligence activities of one nation by means of intrusion of its aircraft into the area of another country can hardly be called a method for improving relations and strengthening trust....

Cold War Politics in America

During his last term as president, Eisenhower tried to walk a fine line on his Cold War policies. Strong anti-Communists wanted to increase defense spending and close the missile gap. Eisenhower was an anti-Communist, too, but he opposed spending more money than necessary on weapons. He cautioned against "the feverish building of vast armaments." He also knew that the missile gap was a myth. The United States had more missiles than the Soviet Union and was improving them all the time. The new generation of weapons included the Minuteman land-based missiles and Polaris submarine-based missiles.

However, in the press and among many voters, the fear of losing the arms race was strong. As the 1960 presidential election

President John F. Kennedy

neared, the Democrats took advantage of that fear. In Congress, Democratic senator John F. Kennedy warned, "Unless immediate steps are taken, failure to maintain our relative power of retaliation may in the near future expose the United States to a nuclear missile attack.... Time is short. This situation should have never been permitted to arise."

A few months after making that speech, Kennedy was the Democratic candidate for president. His opponent was Vice President Richard Nixon. In an extremely close race, Kennedy won. Young and good-looking, Kennedy seemed to have an energy that Eisenhower, Nixon, and the Republicans lacked. Many Americans hoped Kennedy could close the missile gap and revive the country's strength.

Kennedy brought in experts from businesses and universities to run his administration. His choice for secretary of defense was Robert McNamara. But McNamara was no expert on missiles. "I hardly knew the difference between a nuclear weapon and a conventional weapon," he said. "[M]y first responsibility...was to determine the degree of the [missile] gap and initiate action to close it and it took us about three weeks to determine yes, there was a gap. But the gap was in our favor."

Kennedy inherited a number of problems from Eisenhower, though obviously the alleged missile gap was not one of them. In Cuba a revolution had brought a Communist leader, Fidel Castro, into power. In Asia the United States was trying to prevent Communists from taking over its ally, South Vietnam. Among some Third World countries, the United States seemed to be losing influence. And unknown to Kennedy, the Soviet Union was about to score another historic first in the space race.

Circling Earth

Yuri Gagarin #4

On April 12, 1961, a huge rocket sat on a launch pad in a remote part of the Soviet Union. On top of the rocket was a small spacecraft. Inside this craft was Yuri Gagarin. For a year Gagarin and a group of cosmonauts—the Russian term for astronauts—had been training for this mission. Just a few days earlier, Soviet officials had picked Gagarin to be the first human to fly into space.

Gagarin later described the liftoff of his rocket. "I heard a whistling and increasing noise. I felt how the whole body of the giant spaceship started to tremble, and slowly, very slowly took off." Gagarin soared through the atmosphere and reached almost 200 miles (320 km) above Earth. Traveling at more than 16,000 miles (25,600 km) per hour, he made one complete orbit of Earth. The entire flight lasted 108 minutes. When Gagarin returned to Earth's atmosphere, he ejected from his spacecraft. Then he and the capsule parachuted separately to the ground.

At home Gagarin was treated as a hero, and the Soviet Union celebrated another scientific triumph. Said one Soviet citizen, "There were tears of joy. People kissed strangers in the streets." But in the United States, Gagarin's flight was another blow to American pride. Still, Kennedy and his advisors knew that overall, U.S. technology was ahead of the Soviets'. And Kennedy promised that before the end of the decade, the United States would "land a man on the moon and return him safely to earth." The space race had taken another dramatic turn.

Soviet filmmaker Vladimir Suvorov documented the first years of the Soviet space program, including the launch of Yuri Gagarin. Below are some of the notes Suvorov took at the time of Gagarin's flight.

Yuri Gagarin

Now with the service girders taken away, the rocket is shining in all its futuristic beauty among the yellow-brown and bright-blue landscape. At the rocket top, the hatch lid is glittering in the bright sun. Behind, the first man ever going to challenge space is sitting and waiting for his mission to start. Is he destined to return to the Earth safely, or to perish in the infinity of the Universe?...

The rocket now is living a life of its own. It steams, crackles, hisses. In its "nerves"—computers, sophisticated instruments and devices, cables, valves, and pipelines—unseen work is being done....

...In the corridor of the small [communications] building, on its porch and beside the building there are hundreds of people standing, talking, and passing the news to each other. Here are the people who have completed their shifts but do not want to go home, being afraid to miss history in the making.... It is worthwhile to be alive for the sake of this moment!

6

COLD WAR HOME FRONT

During the 1950s and early 1960s, the Cold War dominated the attention of the leaders of the Soviet Union and the United States. The rivalry also influenced the lives of the average citizens of these countries. Civil defense and the sense of competition with an outside enemy were realities of the day. But people were not constantly frozen by fear. Life went on within the two countries and their allied states.

In some ways this era featured better times for many Soviet and American citizens, despite the dangers of the Cold War. The United States enjoyed economic growth that brought prosperity to more people than ever before. In the Soviet Union, the worst aspects of Stalin's rule ended after his death. But things were far from perfect in either country. Not all Americans shared equally in their country's new wealth. Soviet citizens still suffered a lack of freedom, and many still faced poverty.

At times during this period, people from the two ideologically opposed countries came together in peaceful and productive ways. Aside from the diplomatic conferences and contacts, there were some chances for average Russians and Americans to meet. Though limited, these contacts held out some hope for improving Cold War tensions.

An Age of Consensus

When Dwight Eisenhower began his first term as president, the battle against communism was going on overseas and abroad. In Asia, U.S. troops were fighting to protect South Korea from a Communist takeover by North Korea. In the United States, Senator Joseph McCarthy was leading the search for Communist spies and supporters in the U.S. government.

McCarthy used the hunt for Communists to further his own political career. This crusade played on genuine and

Senator Joseph McCarthy (right)—shown here with his assistant Roy Cohn—led the fight against suspected Communists in the U.S. government.

well-founded fears in the country. Since the 1930s the Soviet Union had recruited hundreds of Americans to spy on their own country. But McCarthy's tactics of attacking his enemies and accusing innocent people led to unfounded fears about who was actually a Communist or a spy. McCarthy lost his influence in 1954, and the fear that Communists were controlling the government and universities declined.

However, even an anti-Communist like Eisenhower realized that McCarthy had left behind an atmosphere of distrust. In his memoirs Eisenhower wrote, "McCarthyism took its toll on many individuals and on the nation. No one was safe from charges recklessly made from inside the walls of congressional immunity.... The cost was often tragic." (Congressional immunity gives senators or representatives protection from being held legally liable for anything they say on the floor of Congress while Congress is in session.)

Throughout the 1950s, people who held socialist beliefs or seemed radical in some way were sometimes labeled "un-American." The era is sometimes called an "age of consensus," because most Americans shared—or were supposed to share—the same beliefs. The need to oppose communism was one of those beliefs. So was promoting capitalism. People who did not conform were held up to suspicion. Only a few artists and intellectuals publicly challenged the consensus.

Poets Lawrence Ferlinghetti (left) and Allen Ginsberg look on as Stella Kerouac autographs a book by her late husband, Jack, in June 1988.

Starting in the late 1940s, a group of writers based in New York City began sharing ideas. They were influenced by Eastern philosophy, such as Buddhism, and they disagreed with the larger American culture. These writers included Allen Ginsberg, Jack Kerouac, and William Burroughs. Collectively they were called the Beats, and the people who responded to their writings are sometimes called the *Beat Generation.*

Many of the Beats were poets. They wrote free verse—poems without a set beat or meter—and tried to recreate the rhythms of jazz music. The Beats stressed exploring personal truths in a spontaneous way.

One of Ginsberg's poems was called "America." Written in 1956, it expressed Ginsberg's view of the country during the "age of consensus." One part mocked the Cold War mentality in the United States.

An Age of Affluence

The age of consensus was also an age of *affluence,* or wealth. From 1948 to 1960, the U.S. economy grew at an average rate of 3.4 percent every year. This rate was much higher than the decades before or after that period. More people were able to get better jobs and join the middle class. These people moved out of cities and flooded into the surrounding suburbs. The suburban population grew by 50 percent during the 1950s. People bought cars, televisions, and other consumer goods.

Planned suburban communities such as Levittown, New York, provided affordable housing for many American workers.

Government policies helped fuel the economic growth. A law passed by Congress called the GI Bill let soldiers take out loans to attend college and buy homes. A highway construction boom pumped billions of dollars into the economy. (The highways were also part of Cold War strategy—wide interstates were designed to give Americans a way to escape a possible Soviet nuclear attack.) Eisenhower tried to limit government spending in some areas, but he also kept many New Deal and Fair Deal programs in place. These social programs, begun by Franklin Roosevelt and Harry Truman, provided economic support to Americans who did not share in the new prosperity. For example, new federal funds built 70,000 units of public housing during Eisenhower's two terms.

Despite concerns about spending too much money, Eisenhower increased defense spending. This money helped create the strong economy of the 1950s. Much of the money went for military research and weapons. New technologies such as the computer and the transistor had many military uses. Elliott Katz, a missile designer for the defense industry, said that "the [Soviet] threat opened the door to [the] money vault.... [T]he defense industry and its budgets seemed to be based on the fact that the Russians were 10 feet tall.... I mean our well-being, our sustenance was dependent on the defense industry." The increases in defense spending took off after the Soviet Union launched *Sputnik*. By 1960 defense spending was about $50 billion per year—slightly more than half of the entire U.S. federal budget.

Technology TECHNOLOGY FOR WAR AND PEACE

ENIAC was the world's first computer.

The world's first computer was introduced in 1946. It was called ENIAC, for "Electronic Numerical Integrator and Computer." ENIAC was built for the U.S. Army. It was used to calculate the path of artillery ammunition. This computer weighed 30 tons and was the size of a small house.

Transistors, invented in 1947, helped shrink the size of computers and other electronic devices. They replaced vacuum tubes for amplifying electric signals. Transistors were much smaller and used less power than tubes. A big improvement to transistors came in 1958, with the *integrated circuit*. Many transistors were layered together on a small piece of silicon. These circuits were also called *chips*. In 1962 the U.S. Air Force helped boost the development of silicon chips by using them in computers inside missiles.

Defense spending on computers, transistors, and integrated circuits led to improvements and lower costs. Eventually these technologies became common in consumer goods, from radios to watches and today's personal computers.

The Struggle for Racial Equality

The booming economy was one of America's great achievements during the 1950s. But the country fared less well in protecting the civil rights of its minorities. African Americans in particular still faced legal and economic barriers, especially in the South. President Eisenhower proclaimed, "There must be no second-class citizens in this country." But many blacks were treated unequally.

Court–ordered integration of U.S. schools began in the 1950s and continued for decades. Here Boston police escort school buses as part of a 1974 integration plan.

Starting in the 1950s, African Americans began challenging these inequalities in the Supreme Court. Their first major victory came in 1954, in *Brown v. Board of Education of Topeka*. The Supreme Court ruled that "separate but equal" schools were unconstitutional.

An 1896 court ruling, *Plessy v. Ferguson*, had given states the legal right to segregate blacks and whites on public trains, as long as the races had equal accommodations. The ruling was then used to justify separate schools. In theory the education offered at white schools and black schools was supposed to be the same. In reality the education at the black schools was worse than at the white schools. The Supreme Court said these segregated schools were illegal. Later, laws allowing other forms of segregation were also struck down.

However, enforcing the rulings was not easy. In 1957 Eisenhower had to send U.S. troops into Little Rock, Arkansas, to escort black students into what had been an all-white school. Congress also passed new laws to protect voting rights for blacks. But state governments still found ways to keep African Americans out of the voting booth. Eisenhower knew how strong racism was in America. "It is difficult through law and force to change a man's heart," he said. The struggle to guarantee civil rights would increase in the 1960s, sometimes turning violent.

Sources　　CIVIL RIGHTS & THE COLD WAR

During the Cold War era, the United States government talked about winning freedom for people who lived under Communist rule. But at home the government sometimes did not guarantee the rights of some of its own citizens—blacks and other minorities. Here, Eleanor Holmes Norton, an African American congresswoman from Washington, D.C., expresses some of her views on civil rights and the Cold War.

It was the conformist period...when there was a way to act and a way to be, and the Cold War, and the McCarthy period in particular, reinforced all that. Now, the effect on the civil rights movement was that, until the courts did their job, it is hard to believe that the civil rights movement would have moved ahead at all in the Fifties.... But when the court spoke up...all of the Cold War paraphernalia around the notion of protest fell away....

...[N]o Americans could have been more aware of the contradiction between the pronouncement of American ideals abroad and realities at home than black Americans, and particularly black Americans where this black American lived [Washington, D.C.], in the seat of the leading democratic power in the world.... [T]his notion that this was the land of the free and the home of the brave was a contradiction that black people pointed up at every opportunity.

Change in the Soviet Union

The rise to power of Nikita Khrushchev brought many changes to the Soviet Union. Even earlier, right after Stalin's death in 1953, the Soviet government relaxed some of its most brutal policies. Although the Communist party still held absolute control, the extreme fear created by Stalin had lessened.

The Soviet leaders turned much of their attention to economic change. To Khrushchev the goal was to match and then surpass the economic growth in the West, and particularly in the United States. "You will see," he said, "that communists live not worse, but better than many other countries. In the future we'll live better than any other country."

Khrushchev tried to introduce some consumer goods, such as televisions, appliances, and cars. He also tried to increase food production. Under his "Virgin Lands" policy, some 90 million acres of open land were turned into farmland. Khrushchev also called on Soviet farmers to

Soviet farmers take part in Khrushchev's "Virgin Lands" effort.

produce more meat and dairy products. "The Virgin Lands and Khrushchev are inseparable," one Soviet citizen said. "He woke up the whole country. He inspired people. It was exciting and romantic."

At first the new agricultural plans seemed successful. The Virgin Lands increased wheat production and the new dairy and meat goals were met. But the new farmlands eventually stopped producing crops, and the Soviet Union lacked some of the tools needed for modern farming, such as fertilizers, pesticides, and adequate transportation systems. The meat increases also came at a high price, as the methods used to produce them started to reduce the numbers of Soviet livestock. Despite some economic improvements, many people still lacked enough food to eat.

Khrushchev's policies did not end the poverty found in many Soviet villages.

The economic problems were much worse outside Moscow. The capital city was one of the few places foreigners might visit. Soviet leaders wanted to create the image of a modern, wealthy city. But even in the capital, shortages of foods and common items were rampant. The typical citizen struggled to survive.

Building Military Might

One part of the Soviet economy did not change under Khrushchev. The government still wanted a strong military. The Cold War pushed Soviet leaders to spend heavily on technology related to weapons and space. These demands forced Soviet citizens to endure tough economic conditions. But Khrushchev and the Communist party tried to use the Cold War itself as a way to motivate people to accept these conditions. Vladimir Semichastny headed the *KGB*, the Soviet secret police, under Khrushchev. He said about this era, "The West didn't only harm us. It helped us. Because by frightening us it played into our hands. We could say to the people, 'Tighten up your belts, be patient, we have to wait for a better life and be prepared for the worst.'"

Workers in the defense industry faced extra pressure to work harder and faster. Some workers responded to these challenges. Said one defense worker, "We believed that it was our duty to our motherland, and we worked very hard. A lot of young people worked at our factory.... We had our own committees and we created youth brigades which competed against each other. The best brigades were awarded pennants and trophies."

But not all Soviet citizens welcomed the government's pressure to work harder and make sacrifices. They saw the slogans and awards as part of Communist propaganda. Recent Soviet records show that some people were dissatisfied with the social and economic conditions during the Cold War era. But the people had no say in how the country was run, and any protests they made had little impact.

Places   CLOSED CITIES

During the Cold War, the Soviet Union built whole new cities dedicated to building weapons and doing scientific research. Arzamas-16 and Akademgorodok were two of these special cities.

Arzamas-16 was built on the site of the former city of Sarov, about 250 miles (400 km) east of Moscow. The new city was dedicated to the Soviet nuclear weapons program. The scientists who were sent there earned top wages and received many of the food items and consumer goods that most Soviet citizens lacked. Arzamas-16 was one of several "secret" cities built during the Cold War. The city did not appear on public maps, and the scientists referred to their home simply as the "Installation." In

1990 the Soviet government officially acknowledged the city's existence. Today, Arzamas-16 is once again known as Sarov. The city is still under tight security, as it was during the Cold War.

Akademgorodok was built in the late 1950s as a center for science. The city is located near Novosibirsk, in western Siberia. Its name means "academic town," and the city was modeled after Western university towns. Top Soviet scientists went to Akademgorodok to do research in nuclear physics, mathematics, geology, and chemistry. Just a few years after it was built, the city had 60,000 residents. As in Arzamas-16, the scientists of Akademgorodok received privileges that few Soviet citizens enjoyed.

Social and Political Changes

Along with economic changes, Khrushchev also slightly opened up Soviet society. Many political prisoners were freed, and members of most of the ethnic groups who had been forcibly removed from their homelands were allowed to return. In 1956 Khrushchev's speech attacking Stalin set the tone for these changes, though some easing of the old ways had come right after Stalin's death. The new attitude was sometimes called the "thaw."

One of the changes came in the arts. For the first time under Communist rule, Soviet artists had somewhat more freedom to explore personal issues. Before, their art was expected solely to praise socialist values and the Soviet Union. Yevgeny Yevtushenko was one of the first poets allowed to read his work publicly. He said, "[W]e young poets, a new generation, we were [the] only free voices at the moment...."

This new artistic freedom did not mean Khrushchev was ready to give up communism or authoritarian rule. Still, he let other new ideas and attitudes enter the Soviet Union. Stalin had shut off the Soviet people from the outside world. He did not want them to have contact with democratic values. Khrushchev allowed the first contacts between typical Westerners and Soviet citizens. In 1957 young people from America and other countries came to a festival in Moscow. Recalled Yevtushenko,

> [F]or the first time in my life, my socialist lips touched so-called 'capitalist lips,' because I kissed one American girl, breaking any Cold War rules.... [S]ince the beginning of Stalin's purges, the only visitors in our country were just some diplomats and spies from the West.... And for the first time, we've seen such a lot of foreigners...and people were so happy to see, to feel as a part of humanity, as a part of humanity which was stolen from us...."

In the late 1950s and early 1960s, other aspects of Western culture also came to the Soviet Union, though not with official approval. Young people could secretly tune in shortwave radios to hear rock music broadcast from other parts of Europe, and records were smuggled into the country. Teenage boys tried to narrow their pants legs, which was the style in the West. Special guards patrolled the streets, looking for people dressed in Western style. Yuri Moskalenlo, a teenager at the time, said that if the guards found someone dressed like this, "he was pulled out of the crowd and taken to the militia station, where they cut the trousers, then cut [his] hair...."

Culture ☆ POLITICS AND POETRY

Yevgeny Yevtushenko

Yevgeny Yevtushenko was one of the best-known Russian poets of the Khrushchev era. He wrote both love poems and works that described changing attitudes in Soviet society. He read his poetry in the West, as well as across his own country. Some Soviet leaders disliked Yevtushenko's poetry. Khrushchev, however, gave his personal permission for the publication of one of Yevtushenko's most controversial poems, "The Heirs of Stalin."

The poem was written in 1962. The year before, Khrushchev had made another public attack on Stalin and his crimes as leader of the Soviet Union. Stalin's body was ordered removed from its public resting place, a tomb in Moscow's Red Square, and was buried inside the Kremlin. "The Heirs of Stalin" reflects Yevtushenko's concern that some Communists still admired Stalin.

Fidel Castro (left) and Nikita Khrushchev hug at the UN in 1960.

Khrushchev in Control

Khrushchev himself had many contacts with the outside world. He traveled extensively, including trips to Western Europe and the United States. Stalin had not often traveled abroad, especially to the West. Khrushchev's trips were part of the changes taking place in the Soviet Union. They reflected the Soviet desire for peaceful coexistence with the United States.

Khrushchev's attempt to ease conditions in the Soviet Union was not always popular with other Communists. Some low-level officials tried to resist change. High-ranking leaders went even further. In 1957 a group led by Vyacheslav Molotov and Georgi Malenkov tried to push Khrushchev out of his position as first secretary of the Communist party.

On June 18 the party's leaders met, and for the next three days, they debated Khrushchev's fate. A majority of the Presidium, the highest level of the party leadership, wanted him to step down. Khrushchev then called a special meeting, called a *plenum*, for all the members of the Communist party's Central Committee. This committee would decide whether Khrushchev would remain in power. Khrushchev had gathered his allies to support him, including the heads of the army and the secret police. When the plenum was over, Khrushchev had won. He remained in control of the party and the government.

In the past Molotov and Malenkov might have lost their lives for challenging Khrushchev. But Khrushchev did not take such extreme measures. Instead, the leaders of the so-called "Anti-Party Group" were stripped of their important party ranks. Khrushchev then sent them to low-level jobs far from Moscow.

Khrushchev's reaction to the Anti-Party Group was another sign of the new attitudes in the Soviet Union. But the Communist party still used some harsh measures against its enemies. Khrushchev began the policy of sending healthy people to psychiatric hospitals. Their only "illnesses" were that they criticized Khrushchev's rule. The KGB also played a large role in Soviet life. The secret police spied on citizens and encouraged people to spy on their friends, family, and neighbors. Even with some changes, the Soviet Union remained a police state.

In foreign policy some things also remained the same. Despite the push for peaceful coexistence, Khrushchev was not willing to give up Soviet interests. Relations with the United States rose and fell, depending on other events in the world. In 1961 Berlin once again became a point of conflict between East and West.

Sources · KHRUSHCHEV AGAINST MOLOTOV

During the plenum of June 1957, Molotov criticized Khrushchev for trying to end the group leadership that had developed after Stalin's death. He also attacked Khrushchev's foreign policy. Here, Khrushchev blames Molotov for diplomatic errors and defends his own accomplishments.

Vyacheslav Molotov speaks at a political rally in Moscow.

With our short-sighted policies we drove Turkey and Iran into the embraces of the USA and England.... There was a period in which, as a result of a series of incorrect foreign-policy steps, our relations with [other Communist countries] started to worsen.... Molotov's policy could not but lead to a worsening of relations between states; it would have helped the [West] unite their forces against the USSR....

What is the position of the Soviet Union now in the international arena? On all the core issues of international politics, including issues such as the problem of disarmament and the banning of atomic and hydrogen weapons, the initiative is in the Soviet Union's hands. With our peace-loving policy we have put the [Western] states on the defensive.

7

THE
WALL

T ensions over Berlin dated back to the end of World War II and grew worse as the Cold War went on. After the 1953 crisis, when workers protested the policies of Walter Ulbricht, East Germans continued to flee their country through East Berlin. In West Berlin these refugees could get better jobs and a higher standard of living than in their own country. They could also leave the city for West Germany. Under President Konrad Adenauer, West Germany had become a wealthy country, a respected member of NATO, and a popular destination for East Germans seeking a better life.

Adenauer hoped he could one day reunite East and West Germany as a capitalist, democratic state tied to the West. Khrushchev, however, would never accept this. He and other Soviet leaders feared that a united, capitalist German state might attack the Soviet Union, especially if Germany ever acquired nuclear weapons. Khrushchev wanted a Communist East German state. He also had plans for ending the postwar arrangement in Berlin.

People   KONRAD ADENAUER

As the first national leader of West Germany, Konrad Adenauer helped rebuild his country after the damage caused during World War II. He also created strong relations with the former democratic enemies of Nazi Germany. But Adenauer was not successful in his attempt to reunite East and West Germany as a single, democratic state.

Adenauer was born on January 5, 1876, in Cologne, Germany. He entered politics in his hometown in 1917, serving as mayor of the city. In 1933 Adenauer opposed the rise of Adolf Hitler and his Nazi party. Adenauer was arrested and spent time in a prison camp.

After the war Adenauer formed a new political party called the Christian Democratic Union. In 1948 the Western countries occupying western Germany began to plan the creation of a new state of West Germany. They put Adenauer in charge of the effort to write a new constitution for this state. The next year at the age of 73, Adenauer was named the first chancellor of West Germany. This position is similar to the prime minister in Great Britain.

Adenauer's policies helped link West Germany to the United States and the rest of Western Europe. He pushed for West Germany's entry into NATO and various economic organizations. Adenauer retired from government service in 1963. By then he saw a need for Western Europe to rely less on American power and turn more toward the French. Most West Germans did not support this belief. Adenauer died on April 20, 1967.

Khrushchev's Demands

At the end of World War II, the Allies had not signed a peace treaty with Germany. After the division of Germany became more formal in the 1950s, the Western powers signed their own agreement with West Germany to end their military occupation of that country. In November 1958 Khrushchev proposed that the four countries occupying Berlin sign a formal peace treaty with East Germany. The treaty would officially recognize the existence of the two German states. Berlin would become a "free city" with no foreign armies there. At the time about 12,000 U.S., British, and French troops were stationed in West Berlin. Soviet troops were in both East Berlin and East Germany.

In reality, however, a "free" Berlin would have come under Communist control once the Allies left the city. Because U.S. leaders could not accept that situation, they ignored Khrushchev's demands. In response he issued an ultimatum. Unless the two sides reached an agreement within six months, Khrushchev would sign his own peace treaty with East Germany. The treaty would end the postwar agreement to share control of Berlin among the four former allies, and control of the whole city would go to East Germany. The United States would then have to deal directly with East Germany to gain any influence in West Berlin.

Khrushchev's ultimatum stirred concern in the United States. Martha Mautner, a State Department official, said that "the Soviets themselves were committed to a situation in Berlin that the allies could not tolerate, so...there was no...negotiated outcome that was possible." And if there were no negotiations, there could be conflict. Andrew Goodpaster, an Eisenhower aide, said, "I think we were deeply concerned that this could result in a military clash, that we had troops in Berlin and we simply could not submit to East German control of Berlin."

Some military advisors suggested that Eisenhower should send more troops into West Berlin. But Eisenhower feared that a military response could lead to the use of nuclear weapons. Instead, he consulted with leaders from France and Great Britain and made public promises that the West would not abandon West Berlin. He did not give in to Khrushchev's demands.

In the summer of 1959, representatives from the three Western powers and the Soviet Union met in Geneva. Nothing was settled about Berlin, but by then Khrushchev had backed down from his ultimatum. More talks about Berlin were scheduled for May 1960—until the U-2 incident. Tensions rose again between the Soviet Union and the United States. The situation in Berlin remained unchanged.

One City, Two Lifestyles

Khrushchev's failure to get the Western powers out of Berlin upset Walter Ulbricht, the leader of East Germany. West Berlin was a sore spot for the East Germans. Here, in the middle of a tightly ruled Communist state, was an island of capitalism and freedom. West Berlin had been rebuilt after the war, and by 1960 it was a thriving city of two million people. Its streets had restaurants, nightclubs, and cafes that bustled with nightlife.

In East Germany, Communist officials tried to demonstrate that their country was also doing well. Propaganda films showed productive farms and factories. But in reality the East Germans had few consumer goods and only basic food and housing. The economy was propped up by the Soviet Union. The drastic dif-

East Germans head for West Berlin and freedom.

ference between life in the East and the West stirred a steady stream of East Germans to flee westward.

Sports cars built by Ferdinand Porsche, Sr., (left) and his son were an example of the high-quality goods found in West Germany.

Stefan Heym, an East German writer, described the feeling of the era: "The people in the East looked toward the West with what I might say [was] longing. They would have liked to have the same comforts, the same goods, the same chances.... All you had to do was board a subway and you were in another world."

Most of the people who fled East Germany were young, skilled workers. They included teachers, scientists, doctors, and factory workers. Even those who stayed in East Berlin often chose to work in West Berlin. West German leaders encouraged Easterners to resettle in their country by offering money and help finding jobs. In 1957 East Germany tried to stop the flow of people by passing a new law. Anyone caught fleeing to the West would be sent to prison. But first these people had to be caught, and the odds of avoiding jail were in their favor. Every day up to 1,000 more East Germans left for the West.

Ulbricht kept the pressure on Khrushchev to do something about Berlin. The two men met on November 30, 1960, to discuss the possible results if East Germany and the Soviet Union signed their own peace treaty. By then Khrushchev knew he had a new counterpart in the United States: John F. Kennedy. Khrushchev wanted to wait for Kennedy to take the presidency before making any new demands about Berlin.

Sources ☆ ULBRICHT & KHRUSHCHEV MEET

Here are excerpts from the November 30, 1960, meeting between Walter Ulbricht and Nikita Khrushchev.

Ulbricht: *[T]he situation in Berlin has become complicated, not in our favor. West Berlin has strengthened economically....*

Khrushchev: *We must create the conditions so that the GDR [East German] economy will not be vulnerable to our enemies. We didn't know that the GDR was so vulnerable to West Germany. This is not good; we must correct this now.*

In the political regard, we are almost certain that the Western powers will not start war if we sign a peace treaty with the GDR. Economically, do you think that they will declare a blockade, economic war? I think they won't....

...Politically, our situation would improve since it would mean defeat for the West. If we don't sign a peace treaty in 1961, then when? If we don't sign it in 1961, then our prestige will have been dealt a blow and the position of the West, and West Germany in particular, will be strengthened.... Of course, in signing a peace treaty, we will have to put our rockets on military alert. But, luckily, our adversaries still haven't gone crazy; they still think and their nerves still aren't bad.

Khrushchev and Kennedy

Khrushchev was glad to see John F. Kennedy defeat Richard Nixon in the 1960 election. Soviet leaders generally felt they could get along better with Democrats than with Republicans. Khrushchev eagerly accepted Kennedy's proposal that the two leaders meet in Vienna in June 1961.

Khrushchev and Kennedy meet in Vienna, Austria.

Entering the meetings, Khrushchev seemed to have a political advantage over Kennedy. The U.S. president had been embarrassed by the *Bay of Pigs* affair. This was a failed attempt to overthrow the Communist government of Cuba. McGeorge Bundy, Kennedy's national security advisor, said the new president had his own agenda. Kennedy wanted to show that the United States was committed to West Berlin. "Kennedy, I think, also felt a certain pressure on himself personally to demonstrate to Khrushchev that he was not going to be pushed around."

The meetings went badly. The two leaders first discussed general topics. Khrushchev startled Kennedy with his aggressive manner. The Soviet leader seemed unimpressed with Kennedy's abilities. On the second day, they talked specifically about Berlin. Khrushchev again demanded that the West sign a peace treaty with East Germany and agree to make Berlin a free city. Kennedy said the Americans had a right to remain in Berlin as a result of their victory in World War II.

Said Bundy, "The meeting was unproductive and, the longer it went on, the more that became apparent.... I think President Kennedy was increasingly impressed by the fact that the meeting was not producing any hopeful signals about understanding an

agreement over Berlin or for that matter almost any other subject."
At one point Khrushchev shouted, "I want peace, but if you want
war that is your problem." He insisted that the Soviet Union would
sign its own peace treaty with East Germany within six months.
When the meeting ended, neither man offered to shake hands.

Flexing Military Arms

According to some reports, Kennedy was shaken by the meeting with Khrushchev. Just a few months into his presidency,
Kennedy faced a major crisis with America's strongest enemy.
Even though there was no missile gap with the Soviet Union, the
United States did not want a nuclear war. But Kennedy was not
going to rule out using nuclear weapons. He was not going to give
in to Khrushchev. The president asked his military advisors for all
his conventional military options. Meanwhile, Khrushchev
announced he would increase Soviet military spending, and his
country would begin a new round of nuclear weapons tests.

On July 25 Kennedy finally gave his response to the growing
Berlin crisis. On national TV he said he would ask Congress for an
extra $3.2 billion in defense spending, mostly for conventional
weapons. He ordered an increase in the military draft and sought
the authority to call up more members of the military reserve.
Kennedy also wanted more than $200 million to improve civil
defense. "We seek peace," he said, "but we shall not surrender."

Khrushchev reacted angrily to Kennedy's speech. He saw the
military moves as a threat to wage war against the Soviet Union.
Always quick to talk tough, Khrushchev said if Kennedy started a
war, "then he would probably become the last president of the
United States." But soon after, Khrushchev calmed down. He
realized the West was not going to give in to his demands, and he
was not willing to risk a nuclear war over Berlin.

In his speech, something Kennedy did not say was just as important as what he did say. The president had clearly stated that the United States would defend West Berlin and the West's right to access to the city. But he did not talk about the free movement of people between East and West Berlin. The Soviet Union took that as a signal. Said Bundy, "It is a fact that we were not going to fight about what the Soviets did on their side of Berlin and that it is quite likely that Khrushchev was helped to understand that American position by the July speech."

East Germans were still flooding into West Berlin. Ulbricht continued to hound the Soviet Union, wanting it to take some action. Ulbricht had asked before about building a barrier between East and West Berlin to stop the flow of refugees. Khrushchev and the leaders of the Eastern European satellites had rejected that idea as recently as March 1961. Now they were ready to accept it.

Sources   JFK'S SPEECH ON THE BERLIN CRISIS

Here are excerpts from President Kennedy's speech of July 25, 1961.

In Berlin, as you recall, [Khrushchev] intends to bring to an end, through the stroke of a pen, first our legal rights to be in West Berlin and secondly our ability to make good on our commitment to the 2 million free people of that city. That we cannot permit....

...The NATO shield was long ago extended to cover West Berlin—and we have given our word that an attack upon that city will be regarded as an attack upon us all....

We cannot and will not permit the communists to drive us out of Berlin, either gradually or by force. For the fulfillment of our pledge to that city is essential to the morale of Western Germany, to the unity of Western Europe, and to the faith of the entire free world....

...There is peace in Berlin today. The source of world trouble and tension is Moscow, not Berlin. And if war begins, it will have begun in Moscow....

The First Barrier in Berlin

East German soldiers put up barbed wire, part of the first barricade that separated East and West Berlin.

Berlin
Becomes A
Divided City
#5

Early on August 13, 1961, the loud noises of construction disrupted the quiet of a Sunday morning in Berlin. During the night, workers in East Berlin had begun digging holes for concrete posts and laying out rolls of barbed wire. Soldiers and police watched, making sure no one disturbed the construction—and preventing the workers from trying to escape. Outside the city Soviet tanks waited for the first sign of any major trouble. The first barrier between East and West Berlin was going into place.

The barbed-wire fence stretched out along the entire border of the French, American, and British sectors of West Berlin. It ran down the middle of streets and cut through cemeteries. Berliners had no warning about the fence, and citizens from both sides were cut off from their homes. The East Germans also stopped train service into West Berlin. Robert Lochner, an American journalist in Berlin, saw an old woman searching for a train into West Berlin. Lochner said an officer told her, "'None of that anymore, Grandma, you're all sitting in a mousetrap now.'"

The United States had expected some kind of restriction on movement between East and West Berlin, but the timing and extent of this wall caught the Americans off guard. Colonel Jim Atwood was a U.S. intelligence officer in Berlin. He said, "There was no anticipation, there was no intelligence pre-warning that this was coming down and I don't think that it was leaked in any levels on the other side...."

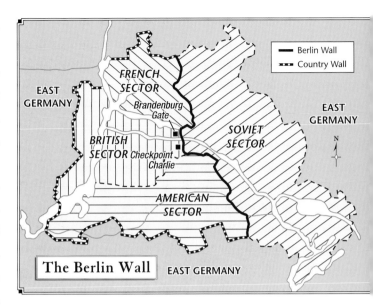

As the barrier went up, people from both sides came to show their anger. Said Conrad Schumann, an East German border guard, "The people were swearing at us. We felt we were simply doing our duty but we were getting scolded from all sides. The West Berliners yelled at us and the Eastern demonstrators yelled at us."

| Places | THE BERLIN WALL |

The Berlin Wall cut through the heart of Berlin. Stretching for 28.5 miles (46 km), the final wall was actually two separate concrete barriers 12 to 15 feet (3.6 to 4.6 m) high. The walls were reinforced with steel, so a car or truck could not ram them down. In between the walls was a concrete road used by East

The result of a failed escape to the West: death

A woman successfully climbs into West Berlin.

While the wall was going up, and for years afterward, many East Germans tried to reach the West. The windows from some buildings in East Berlin looked over into West Berlin, and people climbed down or jumped to freedom. East German officials finally tore down some of these buildings or boarded up the windows with bricks.

Other East Germans tried to climb over or tunnel under the Berlin Wall. Between 1961 and 1989, more than 260 people were killed trying to get around the wall. One of those people was 18-old Peter Fechter. He was shot as he tried to scale the wall, then bled to death as he lay in the "no-man's land" between East and West Berlin.

German border patrols. In front of the walls were barbed wire and steel tank traps. The wall was guarded by gun positions at key points. Automatic guns were also set to fire if someone tried to escape from East Berlin.

From Wire to Concrete

The Wall
Goes Up
#6

Within three days another barrier was added behind the barbed wire: a concrete wall. This was the permanent wall that would separate East and West Berlin for almost 30 years. West Berliners were furious about the wall, and they rallied to protest it. They were also angered about Kennedy's lack of response to the wall. West Berlin mayor Willy Brandt said, "Berlin expects more than words. Berlin expects action."

However, the Americans actually saw the wall as a positive step. State Department official Martha Mautner said that "everybody was relieved to find out that the Soviets had found a way to resolve their problems with the refugees in a way that did not affect allied rights." Still, Kennedy believed that he had to reassure the West Berliners, so

A concrete wall replaces barbed wire.

he sent Vice President Lyndon Johnson and General Lucius Clay to the city. Clay had been the hero of the Berlin airlift of 1948. He later returned to West Berlin as Kennedy's special representative.

When Johnson and Clay arrived, the vice president told the West Berliners, "[President Kennedy] wants you to know that the pledge he has given to the freedom of West Berlin and to the rights of Western access to Berlin is firm." Kennedy also sent 1,500 additional troops to West Berlin. These troops drove through East Germany to see if the East Germans would try to stop them. The American troops were allowed to pass, and they received a hero's welcome when they reached the city.

General Lucius Clay (center) and Vice President Lyndon Johnson (right) in West Berlin. Behind them is West Berlin mayor Willy Brandt.

On August 17, 1961, hundreds of thousands of West Berliners gathered to protest the Berlin Wall. Journalist Flora Lewis described the scene she saw that day.

[The protesters] were determined to march to the Brandenburg Gate [at the border between East and West Berlin], and they were going to force their way through. As I say, it was not really a wall yet; there was armored cars and water-cannon[s] and barbed wire...and troops, but there was not a real wall. They were just going to march through. And [Mayor] Brandt just talked them out of it—it was really an extraordinary performance—and saved what would surely have been a most terrible massacre.... I don't think there was any doubt that the Red Army was going to shoot. Heavens knows what would have happened.

Trouble at Checkpoint Charlie

The East Germans set up only seven points where West Berliners could enter East Berlin. They needed special passes to cross into the eastern half. Other Westerners could enter East Berlin at only one point, a crossing in the American sector called "Checkpoint Charlie." U.S. diplomats were supposed to be allowed through the checkpoint without showing their passports. But in late October, East German border guards refused to let one American pass without first showing his passport.

U.S. troops escort a car through "Checkpoint Charlie."

General Clay, as the highest-ranking American in Berlin, took action. He ordered military jeeps carrying armed soldiers to escort Americans into East Berlin. Colonel Atwood recalled Clay saying, "The Russians understand one thing, and that's force, that's strength. You must never negotiate or deal with the Russians without having a position of strength." Clay backed this up by sending ten U.S. tanks just outside Checkpoint Charlie.

On October 27, the Soviet Union responded. It sent 33 of its tanks into East Berlin, with 10 at Checkpoint Charlie, just opposite the U.S. tanks. Soviet general Anatoly Gribkov said, "Khrushchev ordered the commander of the Soviet troops in Germany that if the West used force, they should respond with force."

The Soviet and American tanks sat 100 yards (91 m) from each other. Gunners on both sides loaded their cannons and waited for orders. Said Atwood, "The tension escalated very rapidly for the one reason that this was Americans confronting Russians." U.S. and NATO forces in Europe were put on alert. So were the bombers of SAC. The situation seemed to be getting out of hand. Finally Kennedy sent Khrushchev a message. The two leaders had opened a secret line of communication just a month before.

Kennedy said that the U.S. tanks would back down if the Soviet forces withdrew first. Khrushchev agreed. Gribkov said, "It wasn't a good enough reason to start a war. Khrushchev himself said, 'We're not unleashing a Third World War because of Berlin.' The Americans realized that too."

The tension at Checkpoint Charlie soon faded. U.S. officials accepted the Berlin Wall, even if they did not like it. Kennedy said, "It's not a very nice solution, but a wall is a hell of lot better than a war." The Berlin Wall became the strongest symbol of the split between the East and West.

Kennedy addressing the people of West Berlin.

On June 26, 1963, President Kennedy came to West Berlin. In a speech to 250,000 people, he assured the citizens of West Berlin that America had not forgotten them. Here is part of his speech.

Freedom is indivisible, and when one man is enslaved, all are not free. When all are free, and we can look forward to that day, when this city will be joined as one, and this country, and this great continent of Europe in a peaceful and hopeful globe, when that day finally comes, as it will, the people of West Berlin can take sober satisfaction in the fact they were in the front lines for almost two decades. All free men, wherever they may live, are citizens of Berlin, and therefore as a free man, I take pride in the words "Ich bin ein Berliner [I am a Berliner]."

8

MISSLES
IN
CUBA

During the Berlin Wall crisis of 1961, Soviet and American tanks faced each other for the first time ever. Though no shots were fired, the situation was tense. The following year the United States and the Soviet Union had an even more dangerous confrontation, this time just 90 miles (144 km) off the shores of Florida.

A poster warns of the danger Cuba posed to U.S. freedom.

Communism Close to Home

Cold War crises first developed in Europe and Asia. By the mid-1950s, they had spread to the Western Hemisphere, as well. In 1954 the United States backed a rebellion against the president of Guatemala, Jacobo Arbenz Guzmán. In power since 1951, Arbenz had Communists in his government and was friendly with the Soviet Union. His economic policies hurt the financial interests of the United Fruit Company, an American business with large land holdings in Guatemala. In May 1954 Arbenz bought weapons from Czechoslovakia. To President Eisenhower and his advisors, Arbenz was pro-Communist and a political danger. The CIA trained and armed Guatemalans who were anti-Communists. In June 1954 these rebels took power from Arbenz.

Five years later another rebellion occurred in Latin America. This time, however, the successful rebel leader was not working with the United States. In Cuba, Fidel Castro led an uprising against Fulgencio Batista. Under Batista, Cuba had close relations with America, but most Cubans lived in poverty. Batista's government was corrupt and sometimes brutal. Taking power in January

1959, Castro promised economic reforms and greater independence from the United States.

Soon after taking power, Castro went even further to distance himself from America. He embraced communism and established close relations with the Soviet Union. Anti-Communist Cubans fled to the United States, and Eisenhower soon looked for ways to eliminate this Communist presence so close to America. Cuba was the new hot spot of the Cold War.

★ People   FIDEL CASTRO

At the beginning of the Cuban Revolution, Fidel Castro was popular with many Cubans, who welcomed his promises of change after the corrupt policies of Fulgencio Batista. But Castro's turn toward communism soon created many political enemies, including the government of the United States.

Fidel Castro Ruz was born in Mayari, Cuba, on August 13, 1926. The son of a middle-class farmer, Castro earned a law degree in 1950 and planned to enter politics. After Batista canceled the 1952 elections and installed a dictatorship, Castro organized a rebel army. The rebellion failed, and Castro was arrested and jailed. After regaining his freedom, another army under Castro's control gained more popular support, and on January 1, 1959, Castro took power.

Castro's calls for economic change appealed to many Cubans—especially poor farmers and the young. But his changes relied on taking control of private property—much of it owned by American interests. This guaranteed that the United States would oppose his rule. He also lost support among some Cubans as he moved closer to the Soviet Union and adopted harsh Communist policies. Castro did reduce economic inequality and illiteracy in his country, but he also set up a brutal regime that violently suppressed personal freedom.

Cuba counted on the Soviet government for economic aid, and Castro kept close ties with the Soviet

Union until its collapse in 1991. Castro also supported revolutionary movements around the world. In the 1970s he sent Cuban troops to the African country of Angola to help Communist forces there in a civil war. Forty years after the Cuban Revolution, Fidel Castro still leads his country, and he remains one of the world's few dedicated Communist leaders.

Places   CUBA

A rather large island in the Caribbean Sea, Cuba was one of the first places visited by Christopher Columbus on his westward voyages. Spain controlled the island for the next 400 years. Cuba became important to the United States after 1898 and the American victory in the Spanish-American War. Taking control of the island from Spain, the United States ruled it until 1902. But even as an independent country, Cuba was mostly under U.S. control, and the United States reserved the right to send in its military whenever it wanted. The U.S. Navy kept a base at Guantanamo Bay, on the southeastern part of the island. (This base is still there today.)

U.S. investors took control of Cuba's sugar and tobacco crops and mining resources. Later, organized crime groups set up casinos in Havana, Cuba's capital. The island became a popular destination for American tourists. Fulgencio Batista took power in 1933 and ruled directly or indirectly until 1959. Under Batista, American financial interests were preserved, while Batista and his associates lived lavishly. The history of U.S. involvement in Cuba led Fidel Castro and his supporters to oppose the United States once they took power.

A Cuban Failure

In April 1959 Fidel Castro came to New York City to speak at the UN. Eisenhower refused to see him. The United States was not eager to deal with Castro and worried about his plans for his country. Eisenhower and his advisors set up a number of conditions

---

Castro had to meet to receive U.S. support. These included no seizure of U.S.-owned land, siding with the United States on international affairs, and keeping good relations with Cubans who were pro-American.

Castro, however, had his own plans, and they did not match the American demands. He executed hundreds of people who supported Batista and the United States. In February 1960 he signed a trade agreement with the Soviet Union. Castro also took control of large U.S. investments in Cuba. Eisenhower responded by refusing to buy Cuba's most important crop—sugar. The Soviet Union then agreed to buy the sugar. Khrushchev was eager to gain a new friend so close to the United States. Said Khrushchev advisor Oleg Troyanovski, "The Cold War was in full bloom. So whatever was unpleasant to the United States was welcomed in this country, and vice versa."

Later, the United States refused to sell petroleum products to Cuba. Again, the Soviet Union stepped in to help the Cubans. The United States eventually halted all trade with Cuba, hoping economic problems would shake Castro's control. The moves merely pushed Cuba closer to the Soviet Union. Said U.S. ambassador Philip Bonsal, "Russia came to Castro's rescue only after the United States had taken steps to overthrow him."

Eisenhower's biggest step against Castro was the invasion of the Bay of Pigs in the southwestern part of Cuba. In March 1960 the president approved a plan for the CIA to arm and train anti-Castro Cubans living in the United States. As in Guatemala, these exiles would lead a rebellion. This rebellion, the CIA believed, would spark other Cubans to overthrow Castro.

Eisenhower left office before the plan was carried out. But President Kennedy was strongly anti-Communist and eager to score a victory in the Cold War. He went along with the plan. On April 17, 1961 about 1,500 Cuban exiles prepared to do battle for their homeland.

The invasion was a military disaster. U.S. airplanes failed in their mission to destroy the Cuban air force, allowing the Cuban planes to attack the invading forces. On land the Cuban army overpowered the rebels, and Kennedy refused CIA requests for direct U.S. assistance. The rebels quickly surrendered, and Kennedy publicly admitted responsibility for the failed invasion. However, the United States was not done with Castro and Cuba.

Espionage   TARGET: CASTRO

Both Dwight Eisenhower and John Kennedy took secret steps to remove Fidel Castro from power. Most of these efforts relied on espionage activities carried out by the CIA.

In 1960 the CIA tried to come up with ways to publicly embarrass Castro. They hoped they could weaken his support among the Cuban people. One plan was to spray a drug into the studio where Castro broadcast his speeches. The drug would make him talk and act strangely. Another effort to make Castro act in a strange manner involved his cigars, which were treated with a chemical designed to make him behave oddly. Apparently, Castro never smoked the cigars.

Castro was known for his long, full beard, and one CIA plan made a target of that famous facial hair. The agency wanted to put a chemical into Castro's shoes that would make his beard fall out. The chemical was tested on animals but never used.

The efforts to remove Castro also included assassination. A deadly poison was added to some cigars meant for him, but there is no record of whether he actually received them. The CIA also talked with organized crime leaders to see if they would help carry out an assassination. One plan was to put poison pills into Castro's drinks.

President Kennedy and his advisors also came up with "Operation Mongoose." This plan to overthrow Castro relied on using anti-Castro Cubans inside and outside Cuba. It also used the CIA to sabotage power plants and other important industries in Cuba. But in the words of Sam Halpern, a former CIA agent, "Mongoose didn't achieve a...thing."

Khrushchev's Daring Offer

After the Cuban victory at the Bay of Pigs, Castro was more committed to communism than ever before. But he believed that the United States was going to keep trying to eliminate him. Soviet leaders also feared a U.S. invasion and did not want to lose their new Communist ally in the Western Hemisphere. Castro appealed for more conventional weapons to fight off a U.S. invasion, but Khrushchev had another plan.

Khrushchev knew that the Soviet Union could not match the number of long-range nuclear missiles the United States had. The Americans also had missiles close to the Soviet Union, in Turkey. If the Soviet Union put medium-range missiles in Cuba, it could match the threat that the American missiles in Turkey posed to the Soviet Union. The Soviet medium-range missiles would also give Cuba added defense against a U.S. invasion.

In July 1962 Soviet ships sailed for Cuba, carrying the missiles, other military equipment, and soldiers. U.S. intelligence did not detect this massive movement of military goods. Said Soviet general Nikolai Beloborodov, "We put all the cars, trucks, and tractors on the top, all the military equipment was hidden under the decks." The Soviet forces in Cuba eventually reached 42,000, and their weapons included bombers, surface-to-air missiles, and tactical nuclear weapons.

By September the Soviet troops in Cuba were preparing launch sites for nuclear missiles that would be targeted at the United States. The Americans now knew that Khrushchev was up to something in Cuba. Kennedy said he believed the weapons coming in were defensive. But he warned Moscow that the United States would not tolerate offensive weapons in Cuba. That warning was too late. By mid-October the missiles were almost ready. A U-2 spy flight gave the Americans their first proof that Soviet nuclear missiles were aimed at the United States.

U.S. troops moved to Florida and placed on alert

Florida

Gulf of Mexico

ATLANTIC OCEAN

Havana

Naval Blockade

CUBA

HAITI

DOMINICAN REPUBLIC

Puerto Rico

Soviet missiles

Soviet troops

U.S. base

U.S. troops

U.S. aircraft carrier

U.S. naval base at Guantanamo Bay strengthened and civilians evacuated

CARIBBEAN SEA

N

The Bomb — SOVIET MISSILES IN CUBA

The Soviet nuclear weapons in Cuba included 48 SS-4 *medium-range ballistic missiles* and 32 SS-5 *intermediate-range ballistic missiles*. The SS-4 had a range of 1,200 miles (1,930 km), while the SS-5 could cover 2,200 miles (3,540 km). Each missile could carry a nuclear warhead with a destructive force of one million tons of dynamite. These warheads were almost 50 times more powerful than the nuclear bomb dropped on Hiroshima, Japan, in 1945.

From Cuba the Soviet missiles could have reached most targets in the United States. Roger Hilsman, an intelligence officer with the U.S. State Department, said, "A first strike would have knocked out all the American air bases, bomber bases, all the American missile bases and all American cities except Seattle, which was out of their range. But Washington, D.C., New York City, Dallas, would all have gone under the hammer."

Kennedy Reacts

Starting on October 16, 1962, President Kennedy and his advisors met to discuss what to do about the missiles in Cuba. The advisors were members of the Executive Committee of the National Security Council—"ExComm" for short. They included Secretary of State Dean Rusk, Secretary of Defense Robert McNamara, National Security Advisor McGeorge Bundy, and Attorney General Robert Kennedy, the president's brother. President Kennedy saw three options: taking out the missile sites alone; launching a general air strike against Cuba; or launching an invasion. On the first day of meetings, the president was sure of one thing: "We're going to take out these missiles."

Cuban Missile Crisis: ExComm Chooses Blockade #7

Later that day ExComm began considering other options, such as talking with Khrushchev and trying to get the missiles out without a military attack. The idea of a *blockade* also came up. During a blockade U.S. Navy ships would patrol off Cuba and prevent the Soviet Union from bringing any more offensive weapons to the island. But a blockade could be considered an act of war. Members of ExComm realized the danger of starting a large nuclear conflict if the United States and the Soviet Union went to war. Said Kennedy aide Theodore Sorenson, "There were no good solutions, every solution was full of holes and risks.... I would wake up in the middle of the night agonizing over what was the right approach, what would work, what would not blow up the world."

As Kennedy tried to decide what to do, he met with Andrei Gromyko, the Soviet foreign minister. Gromyko told the president, "If you don't intend to invade Cuba, Mr. President, you shouldn't worry, because all the weapons are defensive." Kennedy realized the Soviet Union was still trying to deceive the United States about the missiles.

Millions of Americans watched President Kennedy's speech describing the threat of Soviet missiles in Cuba.

By October 22 CIA agents indicated that the SS-4 missiles in Cuba were nearly ready to be launched, and Kennedy had made his decision about what to do. In a televised address, he described his plans for a naval blockade, though he called it a "quarantine." He demanded that Khrushchev remove the missiles. As Kennedy spoke, U.S. nuclear forces went on alert, preparing for war. That evening Rusk told a group of ambassadors, "I would not be candid and I would not be fair with you if I did not say that we are in as grave a crisis as mankind has been in."

Even before the Cuban Missile Crisis, U.S. troops in the Caribbean practiced for a possible invasion of Cuba.

In Moscow, Soviet leaders were solemn as they heard the news. "They can attack us," Khrushchev said, "and we shall respond. This may end in a big war."

Here are excerpts from President Kennedy's speech on October 22, 1962, on the Cuban Missile Crisis.

Neither the United States of America nor the world community of nations can tolerate deliberate deception and offensive threats on the part of any nation, large or small. We no longer live in a world where only the actual firing of weapons represents a sufficient challenge to a nation's security.... Nuclear weapons are so destructive and ballistic missiles are so swift that any substantially increased possibility of their use or any sudden change in their deployment may well be regarded as a definite threat to peace....

...[T]his latest Soviet threat...must and will be met with determination. Any hostile move anywhere in the world against the safety and freedom of peoples to whom we are committed—including in particular the brave people of West Berlin—will be met by whatever action is needed....

My fellow citizens, let no one doubt that this is a difficult and dangerous effort on which we have set out. No one can foresee precisely what course it will take or what costs or casualties will be incurred. Many months of sacrifice and self-discipline lie ahead.... But the greatest danger of all would be to do nothing.

The Blockade Begins

The Soviet Union publicly denounced the American quarantine of Cuba. A report from TASS, the Soviet news service, called the move "a serious threat to peace and the security of nations." But privately the Russians ordered five ships carrying missiles to return to the Soviet Union. Other ships continued to steam toward Cuba. One ship carrying nuclear warheads reached Cuba before the blockade began. Khrushchev said that if any Soviet ships were stopped, his submarines would attack the U.S. ships. The fear of war grew.

On October 24, 1962, the Soviet ships heading for Cuba stopped in the water. Some people in Washington thought Khrushchev had backed down. But President Kennedy was not ready to celebrate. He said, "The game was hardly over." A little later that day, Khrushchev sent a message to Kennedy rejecting all of the American demands. U.S. forces went on their highest state of alert before actual war. U.S. ground troops prepared for an invasion. So did the Soviet forces in Cuba. General Gribkov said, "We would have fought to the last soldier, to the last bullet. There was nowhere to retreat to."

The next day U.S. Navy ships stopped a Soviet tanker. Since it was carrying oil, not weapons, it was allowed to pass. Another ship, from Lebanon, was stopped the next day. It also went through the quarantine. By now both Kennedy and Khrushchev were looking for ways to end the crisis without bloodshed, but also without appearing to give in to the other side.

Espionage — AMERICA'S SOVIET "HERO"

American intelligence officers relied on the services of a Soviet double agent to learn the details of Soviet missiles in Cuba. Oleg Penkovsky was one of the most important spies ever for the United States. A colonel in Soviet military intelligence, Penkovsky first offered his services to the West in 1961. He was upset that his career had not progressed as he had liked. Penkovsky also feared that Khrushchev might start a nuclear war.

Penkovsky was given the code name "Hero" by the CIA. Using a miniature camera, he took pictures of documents relating to Soviet nuclear missiles. He eventually turned over more than 100 rolls of film. Penkovsky's information helped the CIA understand how the missiles in Cuba worked and how long it would take to arm them.

In October 1962 Penkovsky was seen talking to a British contact in Moscow. The KGB arrested him on October 22 and questioned him about his spying activities. After confessing to some of his espionage, Penkovsky was executed.

Secret Negotiations

Cuban Missile Crisis: The Knot Loosens #8

On October 26, 1962, Kennedy received a letter from Khrushchev. The Soviet leader offered to pull his forces out of Cuba if the United States pledged not to attack the island. Before Kennedy could respond, Khrushchev sent a second message. Now he asked Kennedy to remove the U.S. nuclear missiles from Turkey—then the Soviet Union would take its missiles out of Cuba. The U.S. missiles in Turkey were old and easily replaced by submarine-based nuclear missiles, but some of Kennedy's advisors rejected the idea. However, Kennedy said, "Most people will regard this as not an unreasonable proposal." The idea had actually come from Kennedy himself. In a secret meeting with Soviet ambassador Anatoly Dobrynin, Robert Kennedy had brought up the idea of swapping the Cuban missiles for the missiles in Turkey, though the deal could not be acknowledged as a direct trade. Khrushchev had obviously liked the idea (though he preferred to make the deal public).

By this time new problems added to the crisis. A U-2 had strayed into Soviet airspace over Siberia, and Soviet planes had been sent to shoot it down. Hearing the news, McNamara shouted, "This means war with Russia." U.S. fighter planes went out to protect the U-2, which made it back to its base without sparking a dogfight. Later that day, Saturday, October 27, a U-2 was shot down over Cuba. The United States had a standing order to bomb Soviet missiles in Cuba if they took down a U.S. plane. But as Roger Hilsman recalled, "[Kennedy] said don't bomb that anti-aircraft site, I want time to exchange with Khrushchev."

By that night many people on both sides thought a war was at hand. In Washington, McNamara strolled out on a beautiful fall night and thought, "I might never live to see another Saturday night." Fidel Castro later said he believed that "a first strike might take place at any time. I said to myself: If Cuba is in such an unfortunate war, we will disappear from the map."

Castro's concern for Cuba, however, did not prevent him from asking Khrushchev to launch nuclear weapons if U.S. troops invaded the island. During the crisis Castro was the only leader who seemed willing to risk all-out war rather than make compromises. Soviet leaders urged Castro to show "self-restraint."

Early on October 28, Robert Kennedy met again with Dobrynin. Both men knew it could be their last chance to prevent a war. Dobrynin recalled their conversation.

> *He came to me and said: 'The situation is very tense. Your missiles have shot down our plane. Our generals demand that we fight back. If we start bombing, you will start to fight back. What can we do?' I said: 'What about Turkey?' He thought for a while and said, 'You know, if that's the only condition which prevents us from striking a deal, then I'm authorized by the president to say that we agree to it.'*

Soviet ambassador Anatoly Dobrynin meets with John Kennedy at the White House.

Under the deal, the Soviet Union could not publicly discuss the U.S. agreement to pull the missiles out of Turkey. The United States also agreed not to invade Cuba. Khrushchev quickly accepted the agreement. The missiles would come out of Cuba, and nuclear war had been prevented. Castro was not told of the deal, and he was upset when he learned about it. But Soviet and American leaders were relieved the crisis was over.

Khrushchev and Kennedy each thought he had won. Kennedy had removed the Soviet missiles from Cuba without firing a shot. Khrushchev was pleased that the United States agreed to keep from attacking Cuba. The Soviet Union would still have a Communist ally in the Western Hemisphere. Both sides also learned the importance of direct negotiations during a Cold War crisis. They saw the need for avoiding such extreme crises in the future. Khrushchev said the peaceful end to the crisis was a "triumph for common sense."

Sources KHRUSHCHEV'S LETTERS

Here are excerpts from some of the letters that Nikita Khrushchev sent to John F. Kennedy during the Cuban Missile Crisis.

October 26

You are threatening us with war. But you well know that the very least which you would receive in reply would be that you would experience the same consequences as those which you sent us.…

If assurance were given by the President and the government of the United States that the USA itself would not participate in any attack on Cuba and would restrain others from action of this sort, if you would recall your fleet, this would immediately change everything.…

October 27

You are worried over Cuba. You say that it worries you because it lies at a distance of 90 miles [144 km] across the sea from the shores of the United States. However, Turkey lies next to us. Our sentinels are pacing up and down and watching each other. Do you believe that you have the right to demand security for your country and the removal of such weapons that you qualify as offensive, while not recognizing this right for us?

October 28

We are confident that the people of all countries, like you, Mr. President, will understand me correctly. We are not threatening. We want nothing but peace. Our country is now in upsurge. Our people are enjoying the fruits of peaceful labor....

We value peace perhaps even more than other peoples because we went through a terrible war with Hitler. But our people will not falter in the face of any test. [W]e assure our people and world public opinion that the Soviet Government will not allow itself to be provoked.... But we are confident that reason will triumph, that war will not be unleashed, and peace and the security of the peoples will be assured....

Technology — THE HOT LINE

After the Cuban Missile Crisis, Soviet and American leaders saw the value of a permanent, secret communication link between the two countries. This link could be used during any future crises to avert war. The so-called "Hot Line" between Washington and Moscow opened in August 1963.

The first Hot Line was a teletype system. Messages were typed in at one end and printed out at the other. It took about three minutes to type one page of text. Today's system uses satellites and an undersea cable link. Messages are still sent as text, since text is less likely to be mistranslated than a spoken message. Using visible text also gives each side time to think before it replies.

The Hot Line was used for the first time in 1967, during the Six-Day War between Israel and its Arab neighbors. The Soviet Union backed the Arabs, while the United States supported Israel. Moscow contacted Washington to learn if the Americans had helped Israel in its surprise attack on Egypt. President Lyndon Johnson denied any involvement in the war. The Hot Line was used about 20 times during the crisis, as the Soviet Union and the United States made sure they were not dragged into the Middle Eastern conflict.

Time Line

NOVEMBER 1952 The United States tests the world's first hydrogen bomb.

JANUARY 1953 Dwight Eisenhower is sworn in as president of the United States.

MARCH 1953 Joseph Stalin dies; a committee of Communist leaders takes over the Soviet government.

JUNE 1953 Protests in East Germany end with violence, but East German ruler Walter Ulbricht remains in power.

AUGUST 1953 The Soviet Union tests its first hydrogen bomb.

SEPTEMBER 1953 Nikita Khrushchev is named leader of the Soviet Communist party.

JANUARY 1954 Khrushchev announces the "Virgin Lands" campaign, an attempt to reform Soviet agriculture; the United States launches the U.S.S. *Nautilus*, the world's first nuclear-powered submarine.

MAY 1954 In *Brown v. Board of Education of Topeka*, the U.S. Supreme Court strikes down "separate but equal" schooling.

JUNE 1954 Rebels backed by the United States overthrow Guatemalan president Jacobo Arbenz.

MAY 1955 The Soviet Union and its Eastern European satellites form a defense alliance called the Warsaw Pact; the four Allied powers from World War II agree to end their military occupation of Austria; the United States, France, and Great Britain end their military occupation of West Germany.

JULY 1955 President Eisenhower and Soviet officials meet in Geneva, Switzerland. The Americans realize that Khrushchev is the true Soviet leader.

FEBRUARY 1956 In a secret speech at the 20th Congress of the Soviet Communist party, Khrushchev denounces Stalin and his abuses of power.

JUNE 1956 Polish workers and the military clash.

JULY 1956 First flights of a new U.S. spy plane—the U-2— take place.

OCTOBER 1956 Reformer Wladyslaw Gomulka comes to power in Poland; he assures Khrushchev that the Poles will remain loyal to the Soviet Union. Protests break out in Hungary; another reformer, Imre Nagy, comes to power there. British, French, and Israeli forces attack Egypt during the Suez Canal crisis.

NOVEMBER 1956 Soviet armed forces attack Budapest and end Nagy's attempts at reform.

MAY 1957	The Soviet Union tests the world's first intercontinental ballistic missile (ICBM).
JUNE 1957	Khrushchev thwarts an attempt by other Soviet Communists to remove him from power.
OCTOBER 1957	The Soviet Union launches the first artificial satellite, *Sputnik*.
JANUARY 1958	The United States launches its first satellite, *Explorer*.
JANUARY 1959	Fidel Castro takes power in Cuba.
JULY 1959	Khrushchev and U.S. vice president Richard Nixon hold their "kitchen debate" in Moscow.
SEPTEMBER 1959	Khrushchev visits the United States.
FEBRUARY 1960	Castro seeks closer ties with the Soviet Union.
MAY 1960	U-2 pilot Francis Gary Powers is shot down while on a spy mission over the Soviet Union.
AUGUST 1960	The U.S. satellite *Corona* becomes the world's first photo reconnaissance satellite.
JANUARY 1961	John F. Kennedy is sworn in as president of the United States.
APRIL 1961	Anti-Castro Cubans, backed by the United States, suffer a military defeat at the Bay of Pigs.
JUNE 1961	Kennedy and Khrushchev meet in Vienna, Austria, to discuss growing tensions in Berlin.
AUGUST 1961	East German officials construct a barrier to separate East and West Berlin.
OCTOBER 1961	U.S. and Soviet tanks face each other along the Berlin Wall, but the crisis ends without bloodshed.
SEPTEMBER 1962	Soviet military troops begin constructing nuclear missile sites in Cuba.
OCTOBER 1962	Kennedy demands that the Russians remove their missiles from Cuba; Soviet and American forces worldwide prepare for war. The Cuban Missile Crisis finally ends when Kennedy agrees to not invade Cuba and to remove U.S. missiles in Turkey, and Khrushchev agrees to remove the Soviet missiles in Cuba.
AUGUST 1963	The Soviet Union and the United States agree to open a direct line of communication—the "Hot Line"—designed to prevent a future crisis similar to the one in Cuba.

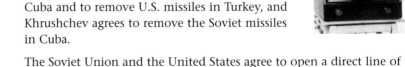

Glossary

antiaircraft—Capable of shooting airplanes or other aircraft out of the sky.

Bay of Pigs—A body of water on the southwestern coast of Cuba; site of a failed U.S.-sponsored invasion in 1961.

Beat Generation—The nickname for a group of U.S. writers who emerged in the 1950s and challenged many traditional American values; also fans of these writers.

blockade—A naval operation that prevents ships from entering or leaving a port.

Bolshevik—A member of a Communist political party that existed in Russia at the time of the 1917 revolution and after; something related to that party and its beliefs.

bomb shelter—An underground room, usually made of concrete, designed to protect against the effects of a bomb attack, particularly a nuclear bomb.

bomber gap—The difference in the number of bomber planes owned by two countries.

capitalism—An economic system that promotes free enterprise and private ownership of goods; individuals and companies, rather than the government, make most economic decisions.

Checkpoint Charlie—In Berlin, a crossing point between the eastern and western halves of the city.

Central Intelligence Agency (CIA)—A U.S. government organization that gathers information about and sometimes influences events in foreign countries.

civil defense—Government policies and plans for protecting civilians during a nuclear war.

closed city—A Soviet city kept under tight military security.

communism—A political system featuring one party that holds complete power and promotes socialism.

conservative—A person who wants to hold on to traditional beliefs or policies.

containment—The U.S. policy after World War II that involved stopping the spread of communism and the influence of the Soviet Union.

conventional weapons—Arms that do not use nuclear energy for their destructive force.

democracy—A government that is ruled by the citizens of a state, who vote on issues directly or elect representatives to decide issues for them.

deployment—The introduction of a weapon to a military force; the strategic placement of military troops and weapons.

deter—To prevent or stop.

diplomat—A government representative who negotiates with foreign governments.

disengagement—The pulling out of military troops from a particular region.

duck and cover—Civil defense tactic that encouraged U.S. children to duck down under their desks and cover their heads with their hands in case of a nuclear attack.

espionage—The process of gathering secret information.

ExComm—Short for "Executive Committee of the National Security Council"; President Kennedy's top advisors during the Cuban Missile Crisis.

fallout—The radioactive particles released during a nuclear explosion.

fission—The splitting of atoms to release the energy stored inside.

fusion—The joining together of atoms to create energy.

Hot Line—A direct communications link between the president of the United States and leaders in the Soviet Union.

hydrogen bomb—A highly destructive weapon that gets its explosive force from nuclear fusion.

ideology—A set of basic beliefs that help shape attitudes or behavior.

intercontinental ballistic missile (ICBM)—A missile that can travel more than 3,500 miles (5,600 km)—from one continent to another—carrying one or more nuclear warheads.

integrated circuit—Transistors layered on top of each other on a chip made of silicon; also called a "silicon chip" or "chip"; see also *transistor*.

intermediate-range ballistic missile—A nuclear missile with a shorter range than an ICBM, usually from about 1,500 to 3,500 miles (2,400 to 5,600 km).

iron curtain—The symbolic boundary between Western and Eastern Europe during the Cold War; also the actual barbed wire and other boundaries separating these two regions.

KGB—*Komitet Gosudarstvennoy Bezopasnosti:* Russian for "Committee for State Security"; after 1954, the name of the major Soviet spy agency.

liberal—A person who wants to promote social and economic reform.

long-range ballistic missile—A nuclear missile that can travel more than 3,500 miles (5,600 km); see also *intercontinental ballistic missile.*

massive retaliation—A U.S. strategy to respond to any Soviet attack with all possible military means, including nuclear force.

McCarthyism—The use of public allegations, often based on rumors, lies, or half-truths, to create suspicion against political enemies, usually Communists; named for Senator Joseph McCarthy.

medium-range ballistic missile—A nuclear missile that can travel up to 1,500 miles (2,400 km).

National Aeronautics and Space Administration (NASA)—U.S. agency in charge of the space program.

National Security Council (NSC)—The body of military and civilian officials that advises the U.S. president on defense issues.

North Atlantic Treaty Organization (NATO)—A military alliance of Western European countries, along with the United States and Canada.

nuclear—Relating to the core, or nucleus, of an atom; relating to weapons that use the energy produced by splitting atoms (fission) or combining atoms (fusion).

nuclear bomb—A weapon that uses the energy inside atoms to create large explosions.

nuclei—The cores of atoms.

peaceful coexistence—A Soviet policy of reducing tensions with the United States.

radiation—Energy released by matter as the result of the movement of atomic and subatomic particles; human beings are exposed to radiation all the time (light and radio waves being two common examples); however, exposure to radiation in high doses or from unusual sources—such as from the explosion of a nuclear weapon—can result in serious illness and death.

radioactive—Relating to the release of radiation.

reconnaissance—A military operation designed to gather information about an enemy.

refugees—People forced to flee their homelands because of war or a natural disaster.

satellite—A country under the influence of a more powerful neighboring country; in space, a natural or artificial object that orbits a planet.

separate but equal—A U.S. legal doctrine that allowed separate public programs and facilities for white and black Americans as long as these programs and facilities were equal.

silicon chip—layers of transistors on a piece of silicon; see also *integrated circuit*.

socialism—An economic system that features government ownership of businesses and a high degree of central control over economic decisions.

Strategic Air Command (SAC)—During the Cold War, the U.S. Air Force unit responsible for the nation's fleet of nuclear bombers.

superpower—One of a small number of countries with a large military force and influence over other countries.

tactical nuclear weapon—A small nuclear weapon designed to be used on a battlefield.

thermonuclear weapon—Another name for a hydrogen bomb.

Third World country—During the Cold War, any nation of Latin America, Africa, or Asia unaligned with a superpower; today, the term denotes an underdeveloped or developing country.

transistor—A small device that controls the flow of electrical current.

Bibliography

The Associated Press Library of Disasters, vol. 2. Civil Unrest and Terrorism. Danbury. Connecticut: Grolier Educational, 1998.

Blum, John, et al. *The National Experience.* 4th ed. New York: Harcourt Brace Jovanovich, Inc., 1977.

Bullock, Alan, and Woodings, R.B. *20th-Century Culture: A Biographical Companion.* New York: Harper & Row, 1983.

Cookridge, E.H. *The Many Sides of George Blake, Esq.* Princeton, New Jersey: Vertex, 1970.

Dallek, Robert. *The American Style of Foreign Policy: Cultural Politics and Foreign Affairs.* New York: Alfred A. Knopf, 1983.

Foner, Eric, and Garraty, John A., eds. *The Reader's Companion to American History.* Boston: Houghton Mifflin, 1991.

Herken, Gregg. *The Winning Weapon: The Atomic Bomb in the Cold War 1945–1950.* New York: Alfred A. Knopf, 1980.

Hofstadter, Richard, ed. *Great Issues in American History: From Reconstruction to the Present Day.* New York: Vintage Books, 1969.

Isaacs, Jeremy, and Downing, Taylor. *Cold War: An Illustrated History, 1945–1991.* Boston: Little, Brown and Company, 1998.

Kennan, George F. *Russia, the Atom, and the West.* New York: Harper, 1958.

Lawrence, John. *A History of Russia.* 6th ed. New York: Meridian, 1978.

Morison, Samuel Eliot. *The Oxford History of the American People. Volume 3.* New York: New American Library, 1972.

Paterson, Thomas G., Clifford, J. Garry, and Hagan, Kenneth J. *American Foreign Relations: A History, Volume II.* 5th ed. Boston: Houghton Mifflin, 2000.

Paterson, Thomas G., and Clifford, J. Garry. *America Ascendant: U.S. Foreign Relations Since 1939.* Lexington, Massachusetts: D.C. Heath and Company: 1995.

Paterson, Thomas G., and Merrill, Dennis, eds. *Major Problems in American Foreign Relations. Volume II: Since 1914.* Boston: Houghton Mifflin, 2000.

Powers, Francis Gary. *Operation Overflight.* New York: Holt, Rinehart, and Winston, 1970.

Shaw, Warren, and Pryce, David. *World Almanac of the Soviet Union.* New York: World Almanac, 1990.

Snead, David L. *The Gaither Committee, Eisenhower, and the Cold War.* Columbus: Ohio State University Press, 1999.

Resources for Students

Books

Allison, Graham T. and Zelikow, Philip. *Essence of Decision: Explaining the Cuban Missile Crisis.* Reading, Massachusetts: Addison-Wesley, 1999.

The American Dream: The 50s. Our American Century. Richmond, Virginia: Time-Life Books, 1997

Cantelon, Philip L., Hewlett, Richard G., and Williams, Robert C., eds. *The American Atom: A Documentary History of Nuclear Policies from the Discovery of Fission to the Present.* 2nd ed. Philadelphia: University of Pennsylvania Press, 1991.

Hill, Kenneth, ed. *Cold War Chronology: Soviet-American Relations, 1945–1991.* Washington, D.C.: Congressional Quarterly, 1993.

Levering, Ralph B. *The Cold War: A Post-Cold War History.* Arlington Heights, Illinois: Harlan Davidson, 1994.

Schefter, James L. *The Race: The Uncensored Story of How America Beat Russia to the Moon.* New York: Doubleday, 1999.

Streissguth, Thomas. *Soviet Leaders from Lenin to Gorbachev.* Minneapolis: Oliver Press, 1992.

Warren, James A. *Cold War: The American Crusade Against the Soviet Union and Communism, 1945–1991.* New York: Lothrop, Lee & Shepard, 1996.

Websites

Argonne National Laboratory
http://www.anl.gov/OPA/news96/news960121.html
This site contains an article called "Lab's early submarine reactor program paved the way for modern nuclear power plants." The article addresses the contributions of the USS *Nautilus* to the future of nuclear power.

Burrows, William E. "That New Black Magic." Air & Space Magazine.
(December 1998/January 1999).
http://www.airspacemag.com/ASM/Mag/Index/1999/DJ/tnbm.html
This article describes the secrecy that cloaked the arrival of the U-2 spy plane.

CNN Cold War
http://cnn.com/specials/cold.war
CNN Interactive online companion to the CNN Cold War 24-part series. Contains program summaries, transcripts of interviews, maps, historical documents, interactive games, and much more information on the Cold War.

Cold War International History Project
http://cwihp.si.edu
This site is home to a broad collection of primary source documents recently released from Eastern-bloc countries.

Cold War Museum

http://www.coldwar.org

Online web museum dedicated to the history of the Cold War. Provides background information, time lines, photographs, and useful links on the Cold War.

Cold War Policies 1945–1991

http://ac.acusd.edu/history/20th/coldwar0.html

This site features an interactive outline of key Cold War Policies from 1945 to 1991. It is housed on the history department site of the University of San Diego.

Concrete Curtain-Berlin Wall

http://www.wall-berlin.org/gb/berlin.htm

This site is dedicated to telling the story of the Berlin Wall, from its creation to its destruction. The online exhibition contains extensive text background information and approximately 100 photographs.

Cuban Missile Crisis

http://www.nsa.gov/docs/cuba/

This site, which is part of the National Security Agency, provides declassified primary source documents and photographs from the Cuban Missile Crisis.

Dwight D. Eisenhower

http://www.ipl.org/ref/POTUS/ddeisenhower.html

This site is housed on the larger Internet Public Library for the Presidents of the United States. This site gives extensive background and links on Dwight D. Eisenhower.

Federation of American Scientists—The High Energy Weapons Archive

http://www.fas.org/nuke/hew/index.html

This site offers a guide to nuclear weapons, including background information, photographs, and time lines that detail the development and use of atomic weapons.

Garvey, William. "New Life for BUFF." Popular Mechanics (March 1999).

http://popularmechanics.com/popmech/sci/9903STMIBM.html

This site contains background information on the B-52 bomber.

Harry S. Truman

http://www.ipl.org/ref/POTUS/hstruman.html

This site is housed on the larger Internet Public Library for the Presidents of the United States. This site gives extensive background and links on Harry S. Truman.

Harvard Project on Cold War Studies

http://www.fas.harvard.edu/~hpcws/

This site contains a wide range of recently declassified primary source documents on the Cold War. The HPCWS promotes archival research in former Eastern-bloc countries and seeks to expand and enrich what is known about Cold War events and themes.

John F. Kennedy

http://www.ipl.org/ref/POTUS/jfkennedy.html

This site is housed on the larger Internet Public Library for the Presidents of the United States. This site gives extensive background and links on John F. Kennedy.

Library of Congress Country Studies—The Soviet Union

http://rs6.loc.gov/frd/cs/soviet_union/su_appnc.html

This site contains an extensive essay on the background of the Warsaw Pact.

Los Alamos High School—Los Alamos/Sarov Sister Cities Project

http://lahs.losalamos.k12.nm.us/activities/sarov

Los Alamos, New Mexico, and Sarov, Russia, are Sister Cities. Situated in each city is the scientific institution that developed its nation's first nuclear weapons. As Sister Cities, the two communities stand side by side to celebrate the end of the Cold War and to hope that the nuclear weapons developed in their scientific institutions will never be used in warfare.

National Reconnaissance Office (NRO)

http://www.nro.odci.gov

The NRO designs, builds, and operates the nation's reconnaissance satellites. In recent years, the NRO has declassified some of its materials, including papers on the Corona satellites.

National Security Archive

http://www.gwu.edu/~nsarchiv

This site contains a broad range of declassified materials obtained under the Freedom of Information Act.

http://www.gwu.edu/~nsarchiv/coldwar/interviews

The complete set of interview transcripts used in the 24-part CNN Cold War series.

http://www.gwu.edu/~nsarchiv/coldwar/documents

The primary source documents referenced in the 24-part CNN Cold War series.

Soviet (Russian) Weapons and Arms Systems

http://www.armscontrol.ru/atmtc/arms_systems/Soviet_arms_main.htm

This site contains information and photographs of Soviet land, naval, and air weaponry and equipment.

Space Race—National Air and Space Museum

http://www.nasm.edu/galleries/gal114/

This special exhibit from the National Air and Space Museum details the history of the space race during the Cold War. Provides excellent background information and images from both sides of the race.

Videos

The Eisenhower Era. Disney Educational Productions, 1997.

Inside the Soviet Union, Vol. 10: The Space Race. MPI, 1990.

The Missiles of October. MPI, 1997.

Index

Pages in italics indicate illustrations or maps.

Adenauer, Konrad 84–85
Africa 26, 30, 120
Akademgorodok 77
Allies 26, 27, 85
Angola 102
Arbenz Guzmán, Jacobo 100, 115
Arzamas 16 77
Asia 30, 64, 68, 100, 120
Austria 26, 27, 38, 39, *89*, 115, 116
Austro-Hungarian Empire 36

B-29 bomber 44
B-52 bomber 42, 43
Batista, Fulgencio 100, 101, 102, 103
Bay of Pigs *89*, 103–104, 105, 116, 117
Beats 70, 117
Beria, Lavrenti 8, 9, 14–15
Berlin 4, 9, 10, *12*, 13–14, 16, *30*, 81, 84, 85–86, 87, 88, 89, 90, 91, *92–93*, 94, 95, 96, 97, *98*, 116, 117
Berlin crisis (1948) 9, 95
Berlin crisis (1953) 12–14, 84, 115
Berlin crisis (1961) 4, 81, 90–91, *92–93*, 94–95, 96–97, 100, 116
Berlin Wall 4, 91, *92*, *93*–94, *95*, 96, 97, 116
Bolsheviks 15, 36, 117
bomber gap 42, 45, 46, 117
Brandt, Willy 94, *95*, 96
Braun, Wernher von 47, 52
Budapest *30*, 35, *36*, 37, 38, 39, 115
Bulganin, Nikolai 8, 23, 30
Bundy, McGeorge 89–90, 91, 107

capitalism 58, 69, 86, 117
Caribbean Sea 102, *106*, *108*
Castro, Fidel 64, *80*, 100–103, 104, 105, 111, 112, 113, 116
Central Intelligence Agency (CIA) 13, 32, 45, 61, 62, 100, 103, 104, 110, 117
Checkpoint Charlie *93*, *96*–97, 117
China 33, 40
Chinese Communist party—see Communist party, Chinese

Churchill, Winston 40
CIA—see Central Intelligence Agency
Clay, Lucius 95, 97
Comintern 11
communism 7, 11, 13, 31, 32, 33, 36, 38, 57, 58, 68, 69, 78, 101, 105, 117
Communist party, Chinese 33
Communist party, German 11
Communist party, Hungarian 35, 38
Communist party, Polish 33–34
Communist party, Soviet 4, 8, 9, 15, 31–32, 50, 75, 76, 80–81, 115
containment 7, 8, 117
Corona 60
Cuba 4, 64, *89*, *100*, 101–102, 103, 104, 105, *106*, 107, *108*, 109, 110, 111, 112, 113, 116, 117
Cuban Missile Crisis 4, 105, *106*, 107–*108*, 109–110, 111–114, 116, 118
Cuban Revolution 100–101, 102, 116
Czechoslovakia 26, *30*, 100

disengagement 53, 118
Dobrynin, Anatoly 27, 111, *112*
Dulles, John Foster 6–8, 13, 21, 27, 34

East Berlin—see Berlin
Eastern Europe 9, 15, 16, 26, 27, 32, 33, 53, 118
East Germany 9–10, 11, 12–13, 14, *26*, *30*, 53, 84, 85, 86–88, 89, 90, *93*, 95, 115
Egypt 39, 40, 114, 115
Eisenhower, Dwight D. 4, 6, 7, 13, 18, 19, 21, 27, 28, 34, 40, 42, 45, 48, 51, 52, 53, 58–59, 60, 62, 63, 64, 68, 69, 71, 74, 86, 100, 101, 102, 103, 104, 115
England—see Great Britain
Europe 9, 15, 16, 26, 27, 32, 33, 39, 40, 53, 79, 80, 85, 91, 100, 118
Explorer 52

Fair Deal 71
France 9, 26, 27, 40, 57, 59, 86, 115
Fukuryu Maru (Lucky Dragon) 25

Gagarin, Yuri 65, 66
Gaither Report 52, 53
GDR—see East Germany
Geneva 27, 28, 56, 57, 86, 115
Geneva Conference 27–28, 115
German Communist party—see Communist party, German
German Democratic Republic (GDR)—see East Germany
Germany 9, 10, 11, 12–13, 24, 26–27, *30*, 53, 84–85, 86–*87*, 88, 89, 90, 91, *93*, 95, 97, 115
GI Bill 71
Gomulka, Wladyslaw 33, 34, 115
Great Britain 9, 16, *26*, 27, 40, 56, 57, 58, 82, 85, 86, 115
Great Terror 8, 15
Guatemala 100, 103
Gulf War 46

Havana 102, *106*
Hilsman, Roger *106*, 111
Hiroshima 18, 24, 106
Hitler, Adolf 11, 46, 84, 114
Hot Line 114, 116, 118
Hungarian Communist party—see Communist party, Hungarian
Hungary *26*, *30*, 35–36, 37–39, 40, 115
hydrogen bomb 18–21, 22, 23, 25, 48, 82, 115, 118, 120

ICBM—see intercontinental ballistic missile
intercontinental ballistic missile (ICBM) 46, 47, 49, 52, 116, 118, 119
iron curtain 39, 118
Israel 40, 114

Japan 7, 18, 24, 25, 106
Johnson, Lyndon B. *95*, 114

Kazakhstan 46
Kennan, George 53
Kennedy, John F. 4, 54, *64*, 88, *89*, 90, 91, 94–95, 97, *98*, 103, 104, 105, 107, *108*, 109, 110, 111, *112*, 113, 116, 118
Kennedy, Robert 107, 111, 112
KGB 76, 81, 110, 119

Khrushchev, Nikita 4, 7, 8, 9, 14, 15–16, 28, 30–31, 32, 33–34, 38, 40, 46, 47, *56, 57, 58*, 59, *60*, 62, *75, 76*, 78, 79, *80*–82, 84, 85, 86, 88, *89*, 90, 91, 97, 103, 105, 107, 108, 109, 110, 111, 112, 113–114, 115, 116

Kim Il Sung 9

kitchen debate *56, 57*, 116

Korea 68

Korean War 4, 6, 9, 43, 62, 68

Kremlin 79

Latin America 100, 120

LeMay, Curtis 24–25

Lenin, Vladimir Ilyich 9, 11

Lucky Dragon—see Fukuryu Maru

Malenkov, Georgi 8, 9, 14, 30, 31, 80, 81

Manhattan Project 19

Mao Zedong 33

Marshall Islands *18*, 25

massive retaliation 8, 21–22, 119

McCarthy, Joseph 68–*69*, 119

McNamara, Robert 64, 107, 111

Mediterranean Sea *26*, 40

Middle East

Minuteman missile 63

missile gap 52, 63, 64, 90

Molotov, Vyacheslav 8, 27, 30, 80, 81, *82*

Moscow 6, 11, 14, 15, 16, 35, 36, 39, 56, 59, 62, 76, 77, 78, 79, 81, *82*, 91, 105, 108, 110, 114, 116

Nagy, Imre 35–37, 38, 39, 115

NASA—see National Aeronautics and Space Administration

Nasser, Gamal Abdel 40

National Aeronautics and Space Administration (NASA) 53, 119

National Committee for a Sane Nuclear Policy (SANE) 49

National Defense Education Act 53

National Security Council (NSC) 28, 48, 107, 118, 119

NATO—see North Atlantic Treaty Organization

Nautilus, USS 22, 115

Nazis 27, 84

New Deal 71

New York City 23, 58, 70, 102, 106

Nixon, Richard *56*, 57, 64, 89, 116

North Atlantic Treaty Organization (NATO) *26*–27, 84, 85, 97, 119

North Korea 68

North Vietnam 64

NSC—see National Security Council

NSC-162/2 21–22

nuclear weapons 4, 8, *18*–22, *23*, 24, 25, 28, 42, 43, 46, 47, 48, 49, 52, 53, 54, 56, 63, 64, 77, 82, 84, 86, 90, 105, *106*, 107, *108*, 109, 110, 111, 112, 113, 115, 116, 117, 118, 119, 120

Open Skies 28

Operation Mongoose 104

Oppenheimer, J. Robert *19*

Paris 58, 59, 60

peaceful coexistence 9, 15, 80, 81, 119

Pearl Harbor 48

Penkovsky, Oleg 110

Poland *26*, 27, *30*, 32, 33–35, 37, 115

Polaris missile 63

Polish Communist party—see Communist party, Polish

Politburo 15

Potsdam Conference 28

Powers, Francis Gary 59, *60*, *61*–62, 116

Poznan *30*, 33, *34*

Radio Free Europe 32, 37

Radio in the American Sector (RIAS) 13

Red Army 96

Red Sea 40

RIAS—see Radio in the American Sector

Rokossvsky, Konstantin 34

Roosevelt, Franklin D. 71

Rusk, Dean 107, 108

Russian Revolution 15, 36, 117

S-5 missile 59

SAC—see Strategic Air Command

Sakharov, Andrei 20

SANE—see National Committee for a Sane Nuclear Policy

Siberia 70, 77, 111

socialism 30, 31, 58, 120

South Korea 68

South Vietnam 64

Soviet Communist party—see Communist party, Soviet

Soviet Union 4, 6, 7, 8, 9, 10, 11, 15, 16, 19, 20, 21, 22, 23, 24, *26*, 27, 28, 30–31, 32, 33, 34, 36, 37, 39, 40, 42, 44, 45, 46, 47, 48, 49, 50, 51, 52, 53, 56, 57, 58, 59, 60, 61, 62, 63, 64, 65, 68, 69, 72, 75, 77, 78, 79, 80, 81, 82, 84, 86, 87, 88, 90, 91, 97, 100, 101, 103, 105, 107, 109, 111, 112, 113, 114, 115, 116, 117, 118

American relations with 4, 6, 8–9, 13, 15, 19, 21, 27–28, 56, 57–59, 60, 62, 63, 68, 78, 81, 86, 89–90, 91, 97, 100, 105, 107, 108, 109, 110, 111, 112–114, 115, 116

Berlin crisis (1953), role in 12–13

Berlin crisis (1961), role in 4, 90, 91, 92, 93, 94, 96, 97

China, relations with 33

Communist party of 4, 8, 9, 15, 31–32, 50, 75, 76, 80–81, 115

Cuban Missile Crisis, role in 4, 105, *106*, 107–108, 109–110, 111, 112–114, 116

Cuba, relations with 101–102, 103, 105, 112, 116

espionage 16, 45, 61, 62, 81, 119

Germany, role in 4, 9, 10, 11, 12–13, 84, 85, 86, 87, 88, 89–90, 91, 92, 93, 94, 96, 97

Great Terror 8, 15

Hungary, role in *30*, 35–36, 37–*38*, 39, 115

Korean War, involvement in 9

Moscow 6, 11, 14, 15, 16, 35, 36, 39, 56, 59, 62, 76, 77, 78, 79, 81, 82, 91, 105, 108, 110, 114, 116

nuclear weapons development and use 19–21, 22, 23, 42, 46, 47–48, 49, 52, 54, 56, 77, 90, 105, *106*, 107, *108*, 109, 110, 111, 112, 113, 115, 116

peaceful coexistence 9, 15, 80, 81, 119

poetry of 79–80

Poland, role in *30*, 33–35, 115

satellites of 9–10, 11, 12–13, 14, *26*, 27, *30*, 32, 33–35, 36, 37–39, 53, 84, 85, 86–88, 89, 90, 91, 93, 95, 115

space program 47, 48, 49–51, 56, 64, 65, 66, 72, 115

superpower, role as 6

Soviet Union continued

thaw 78

thermonuclear weapons development 19, *20*–21, 22, 48, 115

Virgin Lands 75–76, 115

Warsaw Pact, role in 27, 115

Spain *26*, 102

Sputnik *47*, 48, 49–51, 72, 115

SR-71A Blackbird spy plane 46

SS-4 missile 106, 108

SS-5 missile 106

Stalin, Joseph 4, *6*, 7, 8, 9, 10, 11, 12, 14, 15, 16, 30, 31, 32, 33, 35, 68, 75, 78, 79, 80, 81, 115

Strategic Air Command (SAC) 24, 44, 97, 120

submarines 22, 63, 109, 111, 115

Suez Canal 39, 40, 115

Switzerland 26, 27, 56, 115

tactical nuclear weapons 23, 105, 120

Teller, Edward 20, 48

thermonuclear weapons *18–20*, 21, 22, 23, 25, 48, 82, 115, 118, 120

Tito, Josip Broz 30

Tokyo 24

Truman, Harry S. 7, 8, 19, 44, 71

Tu-144 plane 58

Tu-95 Bear bomber *42*, 45

Turkey 26, 63, 82, 105, 111, 112, 113, 116

U-2 spy plane *44*, 45–46, 52, 53, 59–*60*, 61, 62, 86, 105, 111, 115, 116

Ukraine 15

Ulam, Stanislaw 20

Ulbricht, Walter 9–10, 11–12, 13, 14, 84, 86, 88, 91, 115

UN—see United Nations

United Nations (UN) 7, 39, 40, *80*, 102

United States 4, 6, 7, 8, 9, 11, 13, 15, 16, *18*, 19–20, 21, 22, 23, 25, 26, 27, 28, 30, 34, 37, 39, 42, 45, 46, 47, 48, 49, 50, 52–53, 54, 56, 57, 58, 59, 60, 62, 63, 64, 65, 68, 70, 73, 74, 75, 80, 81, 82, 85, 86, 88, 89, 90, 91, 93, 98, 100, 101, 102, 103, 104, 105, *106*, 107, 109, 110, 111, 112–113, 114, 115, 116, 118, 119

Berlin crisis (1948), role in 95

United States continued

Berlin crisis (1961), role in 4, 90–91, 93, 94–95, 97

bomber gap 42, 45, 46, 117

civil defense 23–24, *54*, 68, 90, 117, 118

civil rights in 73–74, 115

containment 7, 8, 117

Cuban Missile Crisis, role in 105, *106*, 107–108, 109–110, 111–114

Cuba, relations with 89, 100–101, 102–103, 104, 105

disengagement 53, 118

espionage 16, 44, 45–46, 52, 53, 59–*60*, *61*, 62, 63, 86, 104, 105, 110, 115, 116

Germany, role in 4, 9, 13, 26–27, 85–86, 89–91, 93, 94–95, 97, 98, 115

GI Bill 71

Korean War, involvement in 4, 6

massive retaliation 8, 21–22, 119

McCarthyism in 68–69, 74, 119

missile gap 52, 63, 64, 90

North Atlantic Treaty Organization (NATO), role in 26–27

nuclear weapons development and use 4, 8, *18*–20, 21–22, 23, 24, 25, 42, 43, 46, 47, 49, 52, 53, 56, 59, 90, 105, 106, 111, 112, 115

poetry of 70

Soviet relations with 4, 6, 8–9, 13, 15, 19, 21, 27–28, 56, 57–59, 60, 62, 63, 68, 78, 81, 86, 89–90, 91, 97, 100, 105, 107, 108, 109, 110, 111, 112–114, 115, 116

space program 48, 49, *51*–53, 56, 60, 65, 116, 119

superpower, role as 6

thermonuclear weapons development *18*–20, 23, 25, 115

Vietnam War, involvement in 24, 43

Washington, D.C. 6, 7, 74, 106, 110, 111, 114

USSR—see Soviet Union

Vanguard rocket 51–52

Vienna *89*, 116

Vietnam 24, 64

Vietnam War 24, 43

Virgin Lands *75*–76, 115

Warsaw 27, *30*, 34

Warsaw Pact 26, 27, 38, 115

Washington, D.C. 6, 7, 74, 106, 110, 111, 114

West Berlin—see Berlin

Western Europe 26, 39, 80, 85, 91, 118

West Germany 9, 11, 26–27, *30*, 53, 84–85, *87*, 88, 91, 115

World War I 11, 36

World War II 6, 7, 9, 11, 18, 20, 24, 25, 26, 27, 28, 36, 37, 43, 46, 47, 61, 84, 85, 86, 89, 115, 117

Yevtushenko, Yevgeny 78, 79–80

York, Herbert 42, 45, 51–52

Yugoslavia 26, 30, 39